Pipes, Kukris and Nips

Pipes, Kukris and Nips

by

Lieut-Colonel G. M. Forteath, D.S.O., M.B.E. (Retired)

The Pentland Press Ltd
Edinburgh · Cambridge · Durham

First published in 1991 by
The Pentland Press Ltd.
Brockerscliffe
Witton le Wear
Durham

ISBN 1 872795 07 2

Typesetting by Spire Origination, Norwich
Printed and bound in Britain by Antony Rowe Ltd, Chippenham, Wiltshire.
Jacket design by Geoff Hobbs

This book is dedicated to my wife
Joan Ross Burnett,
who had to suffer all the lack
of information about my whereabouts
which is inevitable in war

List of Illustrations

List of Maps

Contents

Introduction

I decided that I would not attempt to put my memoirs on paper, until I knew that most of the chief characters were dead. For the same reason I have mentioned very few names for fear of causing widows and others, any kind of 'sad memory' or anger.

Some of the people concerned, who may be alive, will I hope forgive me if they recognise themselves.

In war, one meets many splendid men, and often arranges to meet them again, when peace returns. In the event, they return to their normal work and we to ours, and thus very few ever meet again.

Should any of my wartime friends ever read this book, will they please remember to contact me, who is still proud to have known them.

It is not my intention to describe the various battles in detail or the planning necessary for such operations, or for the long distance patrols, which were carried out. Detailed accounts can be found in official histories.

The story in this book describes the thoughts, humour, and many different tasks, carried out by an ordinary Officer of the old Indian Army.

An Officer carried out his duties without fear or favour, but with considerable affection and fairness. It mattered not to a British Officer what religion was concerned. The men expected us to know their customs and to honour their religious beliefs.

Thus a mutual trust was built up. All this is in the past, never to be replaced.

Abbreviations and Words Used in this Story

Bn.	Battalion
Bde.	Brigade
Div.	Division
Lance Naik	Lance Corporal
Naik	Corporal
Havilder	Sergeant
B.O.	British Officer
G.O.	Gurkha Officer
I.O.	Indian Officer
Jem.	Jemedar
Sub.	Subhedar
S.M.	Subhedar Major
S.C.	Staff Captain
Q.M.	Quartermaster
I.O.	Intelligence Officer
Bde. T.O.	Brigade Transport Officer
B.O.W.O.	Brigade Ordnance Warrant Officer
Tpt.	Transport
M.T.	Motor Transport
O.P.	Observation Post
R.A.P.	Regimental Aid Post
M.O.	Medical Officer
Fd Amb.	Field Ambulance
M.D.S.	Main Dressing Station
C.C.S.	Casualty Clearing Station
Bty.	Battery
Mor.	Mortar
L.M.G.	Light Machine Gun
M.G.	Machine Gun
Hows	Howitzer
Kukri	Weapon carried by Gurkhas
Dar	Weapon carried by Burmans
Nips	Our name for the Japanese
Chlota Peg	Small whisky
Gharri	Horse-drawn Carriage
J.I.F.S.	Japanese Inspired Forces or I.N.A.
K.H.U.D.	Steep Drop in the Hills

Chapter 1

Introduction to the Army

I was born in 1909 at Port Blair in the Andaman Islands, where my Father's ship was engaged in charting the Bay of Bengal and other parts.

My Mother and I were sent to England in 1914 and arrived before the Great War broke out, and settled in Southsea, where there were soon many naval wives, separated by nature of their husbands' service careers.

In 1918 I was sent to preparatory school in Sussex, where I was when the war ended. I can remember the Head Master announcing to the school that the Armistice had been signed and that the rest of the day would be a holiday, and that the School O.T.C. would carry out a route march! We had wooden rifles and an ex-naval Petty Officer used to teach us rifle drill — I hope the Kaiser was impressed! For some unknown reason we called the retired Petty Officer 'Sergeant'. Part of his duties was to take punishment drill on Fridays. He must have been fcd-up with the sight of my face as I was a regular attendant at his parades for the first two or three years at school.

My Mother went out to India to join my Father in the early Spring of 1919. My Grandmother was made by Guardian, she and two of my Aunts had moved from Scotland in order to be near old Elgin friends. They had settled into a very nice house in Fleet.

I now found myself, as many did in those days, wondering where I should be for the next school holidays.

I was very fond of my Grandmother and felt happy and secure with her. I am sure, that those who did not experience what it was like to be a son of a 'Service Family' cannot understand the mood in the country in the early years of this century when we had an Empire. We learnt that our main duty was to the Empire and if necessary we must die for it. I was no different from most of my friends and I was expected to enter one of the Services. Luckily, after the usual childish wishes of wanting to be a member of every profession which was 'outdoors', I wanted to be a member of one of our Armed Services.

I soon found out that the regiment I wanted to join required an officer to have a private income. My Father having lost his inheritance and savings through the actions of a well known financier of the time, meant that I had no income of my own and would have to live on my pay.

I tried for, and obtained, a King's Indian Cadetship which was largely given because of one's Father's career and service. I had decided to follow my family tradition and join the Indian Army.

After I had left my Public School, which was the Imperial Service College (now amalgamated with Haileybury College), I entered the Royal Military College, Sandhurst, as a Cadet en route to becoming an Officer of the Indian Army and hoping to join the 2nd Gurkhas or any Gurkha Rifle Regiment.

After a course at Sandhurst of eighteen months I was commissioned on the 29th August, 1929. Shortly after I had received my Commission I was ordered to embark at Southampton on H.M.T. *Somersetshire*. There was just enough time to accept two great honours for the 2nd Lieutenant and I have never forgotten them.

As a boy at preparatory school I had spent some of my holidays with my Mother's youngest sister who was married to a Naval Surgeon and lived in Southsea. At that time my uncle was Medical Officer to the Royal Marine Artillery Barracks at Eastneigh. The Royal Marines had kindly allowed me to use their swimming pool and the Adjutant and everyone else did all they could to entertain a small boy. I was present at the parade when the Royal Marine Artillery and the Royal Marine Light Infantry were amalgamated.

Many years later the Adjutant I knew was a Major. I had seen him once or twice as he had been at the same public school. When I went to Sandhurst he told me, that as soon as I was commissioned he would ask me to be his guest at Eastneigh. My uncle, in the meantime, was again stationed in the Southsea area and had a sister married to a Naval officer who had just left the Gunnery School where he had been an instructor. This Officer was to play a prominent part in the Battle of the River Plat.

I was asked to dine with the Royal Marines, a great honour which I never forgot. The Naval Gunnery School were giving a dance at about the same time for which I received an invitation.

Towards the end of September 1929, I sailed for India on board H.M.T.

Somersetshire from Southampton together with several young officers who, like myself, were bound for the Indian Army. We also carried a Cavalry Regiment as far as Port Said. At Suez we embarked a different Cavalry Regiment due for India. On arrival at Southampton Docks I was told that the Embarkation Officer wished to see me. I reported to this Officer and was asked why I had an acid substance in my 'hold' baggage? I told him that I had nothing of this sort, which my Father confirmed. Nothing further was said and I went aboard.

I shared a cabin with three other U.L.I.A. Officers, two of them I had known at Sandhurst. The next-door cabin was occupied by a Captain in a Yorkshire Regiment, his wife and young baby. My parents knew the parents of the girl and had met them at Port Blair.

We spent the first night at Southampton and sailed the next day about lunchtime.

One day several of us were sitting in the bar/lounge playing *Vingt et Un* when the Adjutant spotted us and we were curtly told that only Bridge was allowed to be played in an Officers' Mess. Lesson one had been learnt!

Off the Adriatic we ran into a storm and were thrown about quite a lot. I remember the storm as it was my 'Tour of Duty' as 'Officer of the Watch' or Orderly Officer. The troop decks were by now very hot and the men were having a very dismal time.

However, we all recovered but it meant that our troop ship was delayed.

We arrived at Port Said on 1st October, 1929, my twentieth birthday which I celebrated with all on board by a route march around Port Said. When we returned on board I was looking over the deck rail at the shore when a Scuttle to the kitchens was opened and a number of Egyptian coolies were hailed. As they approached they were met by a shower of potatoes. A missionary and his wife were standing close to me and the wife cried out, 'Look what our wicked men are doing'. A short while after this remark the coolies received a handful of coins, so all was worthwhile.

That afternoon the Officers were allowed ashore and I and some friends headed for an hotel at the entrance to the Suez Canal, to celebrate my birthday.

We had a look at the shops in Port Said, and in spite of the short route march we were glad to stretch our legs after our time at sea.

Those who had been celebrating with me decided that we should have a race back to our ship, in the local horse-drawn carriages. Two were selected and we got in. The winners were to receive a bottle of champagne.

My carriage was leading, but just as we approached the British sentry at the dock gates, our traces broke, the horse fell (but was not hurt) and we were deposited at the feet of the sentry. We learnt a lot of old soldier's words and what he thought of our behaviour, the first of many tickings-off we were to get from the men. However, they were politely given.

The storm I have mentioned meant that we docked at Bombay on a Sunday and we, being very young and raw, wondered how we were going to get any money for our journey up-country to the British Regiment, which was to be our home for the next year. Various representatives of banks came aboard, but I could find no-one from the bank I had sent money to from England. However, I spotted one, who I knew and who had been to the same preparatory school. I told John the sad story and his reply was, 'That does not matter, we all work together, how much would you like?' We fixed a sum and I received my first rupees.

The custom was that young Officers intended for the Indian Army should spend their first year in India attached to a British regiment. They were known as U.L.I.A. (Unattached List of the Indian Army). I have met several who hated their year but I was destined to be lucky and spent my year with a first-class Regiment and was very happy.

I received my travel orders and told to catch the Peshawar Mail and to change at Delhi, thereafter to catch the train at about 2200 hours for Dehra Dun, arriving at 0700 hours the next day.

An old friend of my parents met the ship at Bombay and took me to the Yacht Club for an excellent Sunday curry lunch. At lunch I met a young girl who told me that one of the things I would love about India was that there were no fireplaces. A few days later I remembered her words as I froze to death in my tent!

After lunch I was taken 'sightseeing' around Bombay, then somewhere for dinner before catching the G.I.P. mail train for Delhi — two nights' and a day's journey away.

I was now on the way to report to the 1st Battalion The Black Watch (R.H.) and it was up to me to get there.

Chapter 2

U.L.I.A.

While I was waiting for the Dehra Dun train to start, I noticed two Black Watch men trying to find a seat. As I had a four-berth compartment to myself I told them to get in to my carriage. I learnt a lot about the Regiment and subsequently learnt, that both soldiers had just been released from a spell in Military Prison.

I was met at Dehra Dun by a Subaltern who took me out to the Battalion, who were under canvas at Ghangora about five miles from Dehra Dun. The camp was close to an Indian Mountain Battery Lines. The Black Watch Officers' Mess was in a bungalow, some 600 yards from the main camp. The Commanding Officer lived in the Mess as did two very senior Majors, the rest of the Officers were in tents. I was given my tent and I met my Bearer (Shaffie-Ulah) then taken to the Mess for breakfast. After breakfast I reported to the Adjutant and met the C.O. I was then taken to meet the Company Commander of 'A' Company, a Major whose home was near the Moray town of Forres and was some eleven miles from my own family home at Newton, Alves in Moray. So he knew who I was. He was a great character and I never met an officer or man who did not like him.

He was my Company Commander for about six months, then retired to his estate. I soon met all the Platoon Commanders and found myself Commanding No. 4 Platoon, A Company, The Black Watch. In those days there were Four Platoons in each Rifle Company. A Battalion consisted of H.Q. Company, four Rifle Companies and a M.G. Company plus Signallers and Pioneer Platoons who were part of H.Q. Company. The Medium Machine Guns were carried by mules, led and looked after by a Platoon of Indian Army men under an Indian Officer. Each British Battalion had an Indian Platoon attached to its Machine Gun Company.

About ten days after my arrival, the next U.L.I.A. Officer arrived, who had been at both school and Sandhurst with me. We had one other attached Officer at the time, a Royal Marine, who was transferring to a Gurkha Battalion and was many years senior to us. Six months before my year's attachment was due to finish, a third U.L.I.A. Officer arrived.

The Black Watch were stationed at Chakrata, a station situated in the Himalayas. Chakrata was deep in snow during the Winter, so any form of training was impossible and the Battalion marched down to Ghangora for the Winter and for training at the Selected Brigade Camp. They then spent a further three days marching back to Chakrata for the Summer months. These were the days when we marched everywhere and thought nothing of it.

On the march to Brigade Camp we met a Battalion of Gurkhas who had just spent two years in the Khyber Pass and were marching to Dehra Dun, their Home Depot. Our C.O. said that he intended to call on the 9 G.R. and that we U.L.I.A. Officers would go with him. That evening I met the man who was to be my father-in-law about nine years later. I had already met his elder daughter, Joan, at a tennis tournament at the Dehra Dun Club, about a month after my arrival in India.

The Brigade Commander's wife had asked Joan to be kind to two very young Officers, who were attached to the Black Watch.

During the Winter, while we were at Ghangora, the Black Watch held a ball at the Railway Staff College. A Senior Major had been left at Chakrata in command of the Station, a few men and the families. In order to allow this Major and his wife to attend the dance, I was sent up to Chakrata for a night; the other U.L.I.A. Officer remained at Ghangora as Orderly Officer. The road to Chakrata was a hill road controlled by a police post at Saiha, where the 'up' traffic passed those coming down. This was the system on most of the roads to hill stations. The roads were narrow and far too dangerous for two lines of traffic. After a run of about half an hour you reached what was called the Kialana Neck. Here you turned left for Chakrata or right for Kialana, which was a military hill station for British troops and families from stations in the plains during hot weather.

When I reached Chakrata, I found deep snow. I spent the night in the Major's bungalow where everything had been laid on for my comfort. After carrying out the normal duties I went to have a look at the Wet Canteen and there met some real old soldiers who always sat at the same table.

A glass of beer was waiting for the Orderly Officer! I enjoyed my talk with these very long-service soldiers, thanked them and returned to an excellent dinner. The next day I returned to Ghangora.

When the time came, we left Ghangora for Chakrata by line of march. The first day I found myself in charge of the Baggage Guard. Baggage was loaded in bullock carts and it was a hot and dusty twelve-mile march to our first camp. The next day someone else was in charge of baggage and we marched to Saiha where we spent the night.

On the third day we took a shortcut up a steep track and reached the Kialana Neck. The transport wagons continued up the main road, except the mules who marched with us. I soon learnt that a mule, when trained, was capable of following a man so long as the man did not have to use his hands to climb up a hill.

When we reached Chakrata it was snow free and somewhat changed since I last saw it. It was a pretty place with wonderful views of the very high Himalayan peaks and the everlasting snows. The main parade ground contained a full-sized football ground. There was no grass, so a fall meant a grazed knee which had to be dealt with at once, iodine and gentian blue were always at hand. As the weeks passed numerous fruit trees blossomed and produced fruit such as apricots and lychees. Wild flowers grew in profusion, the commonest being Cosmos.

We carried out our normal duties and spent our allotted period on the rifle ranges. We played football and kept fit by the occasional Khud March which meant a 'walk' down the hillside to a valley then back again. Dogs were allowed on these marches and one saw dogs of every breed and those of no known breed. The men enjoyed these marches as they were a change from routine. The hard drinkers were soon spotted!

My fellow U.L.I.A. Officer and I shared a quarter (with fireplaces) and we decided that we would like to have a dog, so we obtained permission to follow up a notice in the Mess advertising Cocker Spaniel puppies at an estate near Fathepur, which was not far away on the Plains below Saiha.

We chose a pup each. Mine I named Bruce, a grand little dog that quickly learned the duties of a gun dog.

The kind people who owned this estate lent us a couple of rods and introduced us to fishing for Mahseer. We were taken to a place called Kulhal, which was at the junction of the rivers Arsan and Jumna. The pool at Kulhal was known to hold some very large fish, both Mahseer and a fish called a Goonch. A Black Watch Officer and his forestry friend set out to try for something big at Kulhal. They made up special tackle and were spinning a two-pound dead bait.

Result — a Goonch weighing just over 100 pounds! They are very ugly fish who eat anything they could swallow, but were quite harmless to human beings!

Because of the risk of that terrible disease, rabies, the number of dogs in a battalion had to be strictly controlled. I was made Battalion Dog Officer and had a number of duties I hated, but strays had to be kept down at all costs. During my service in India I had to have the anti-rabies injection on three occasions. It was no joke in the old days. Neither is rabies, for which there is no cure and the inevitable death is both prolonged and painful. There was plenty for the officers to do at Chakrata, but the men had very little choice. I played a lot of football with my Platoon, also tennis at the club. For those of us learning polo there was a three-a-side polo ground at Kialana and there was trekking and shooting big game in the Himalayas. On Sundays we used to collect a packed lunch from the Mess and go for a very long walk with our dogs, which had to be kept close to us because of panther.

In the days I refer to, we had visits from concert and theatrical parties. One such company came from an island in the East Indies and their posters advertised topless female dancers! However, when the company produced their show everyone was fully clothed. There was a near riot!

Towards the end of the monsoon we were given permission to take two weeks' leave. We were joined by another U.L.I.A. friend whom we met on the mail train at Saharanpur. A friend of ours in the Black Watch joined us. We had decided to spend our leave at Dalhousie, a hill station above the Kulu Valley. My Black Watch friend and I decided to live in the rest house, which was cheap and comfortable. The other two went to stay with friends, who they knew at Sandhurst.

My Godmother had a daughter in Dalhousie who was staying with relations.

At Dalhousie we were made Honorary Members of the Club and soon met other Officers of British Battalions who were 'in the hills' for a hot weather break. They were stationed a few miles below Dalhousie on the main road. This road was a typical hill road, with steep Khuds often 1,000 feet or more, narrow and dangerous.

I met a man whose home was about 600 yards from my family home in Scotland. He was in the General's Personal Staff. The General also came from the same area and had been at day school with my Father.

We were invited, all four of us, to play rugger with the other soldiers on a ground below Dalhousie. We hired a taxi to take us down and enjoyed a good game.

On our way back, we were following a military vehicle, which was carrying other ranks who had been playing in the same game. The road was two-way but narrow and the Khud was very steep. The Khud side was rocky and covered with shale. A few trees grew in this area of the Khud. Our Indian taxi driver considered it safe to pass the military vehicle, so he did so, but in order to be on the correct side of the road before the next bend, he cut in too quickly and hit a front wheel of the truck, thus turning it to the left and towards the Khud. There was nothing the military driver could do and we had the terrible sight of a truck load of soldiers leave the road and fall down the Khud.

We jumped out of our taxi and ran to see what had happened. To our amazement we found that the bonnet had come to rest on the only tree between it and the bottom of the Khud, some 1,000 feet below. We scrambled down the slope and found that only one man had been hurt.

He had jumped out of the back of the truck and had cut his thigh on the shale. As soon as we had got all the men out we scrambled uphill again and returned to Dalhousie, knowing it was our driver's fault and having learnt what not to do when driving on hill roads, and thankful that there was no loss of life.

In the Black Watch, the Orderly Officer for Monday had Church Parade Duty to carry out on Sunday. It was his duty to parade and march the Roman Catholics to Church. It so happened that my Orderly Officer duties often fell on a Monday. The first time I marched the Roman Catholics to Church the jovial priest in charge said to me, 'You don't want to attend the Service, so make yourself comfortable in my bungalow'.

Amongst the priest's books was an English translation of the Koran, which I read and studied with great interest. After having read this book I had a strong desire to learn more about the religions of India and in the course of time was either given books, or purchased them myself.

I believe that the knowledge I acquired may have saved me from making some of the errors which a lot of Europeans made, without any intention or desire to do so, and thus causing offence to many followers of Hinduism, Moslems or Sikhs.

I have mentioned polo at Chakrata. The polo ground had no grass and was covered in sand. My pony, which I had bought through the Polo Fund and had not been fully paid for, died of sand colic. The Officer from whom I had purchased the pony had left the Battalion and was attending a course at the Staff College, Camberley. Someone wrote and explained what had happened. An immediate reply came back which said, 'I hope that Forteath will have better luck in the future, please tell him the deal is now closed. I do not want the balance of payment.' I never forgot such a generous gesture, but it was not until after the War of 1939–1945, when the Officer concerned was a General, that I was able to thank him in person.

During the time in Chakrata I saw my first swarm of locusts. They flew over our quarters and down to the plains in their millions.

During the year's attachment most U.L.I.A. Officers had to spend a week with the Gurkha or Indian Regiment of their choice. This was to enable the Officers, with whom we hoped to live, to get to know us other than on parade. I was asked to spend such a week, met the Officers of both Battalions, who are still my great friends or, I should say, those who are still alive, as many were killed in the late war and several died of various causes. I left Dehra Dun, hoping that I had not dropped too many bricks and would be accepted.

About a month before our year was up our postings came through. I was to report to the 2nd Battalion, 2nd Gurkhas at Dehra Dun and my U.L.I.A. friend to another Gurkha Battalion, stationed elsewhere, I forget now where it was stationed.

Just before we left Chakrata, my friend and I celebrated my twenty-first birthday at the club with a dinner of baked beans on toast! We applied for a week's leave, both from the Black Watch and our new regiments. We spent a happy week, living in a tent on the banks of the river Arsan, at a place called Fathepur, well upstream from Kulhal. We caught a number of fair-sized Mahseer, which were good to eat. We knew the place, as we had tried to spend a long weekend there during the Summer but had been recalled due to Gandhi.

After our week we left for our new battalions. I travelled to Dehra Dun by car and my friend by car to catch a train at Saharanpur to his new destination.

I had left early and reported to the Adjutant in the Battalion office, met the C.O. and was taken to lunch in the Mess by my life-long friend, then shown my quarters which my Bearer had already found and everything was unpacked and ready for me. Such was life in the old India!

I look back to the year spend with the Black Watch with great pleasure but must admit that I longed to be a full member of a Regiment, not just attached to one.

The Black Watch Officers and men were very kind and taught me a lot which remained within my memory, as it did not altogether apply in the Indian Army, but nevertheless taught discipline and pride to be an Officer. There was only one Officer I did not like but I never met him again after my year. I have met several of the others, either at my son's Public School or in the Army, and found them to be just as pleasant.

Those days were well before the Belisha reforms. The Senior Subaltern was someone to be reckoned with, many of whom had sixteen or seventeen years service.

There were very many funny events which I could recount of my first year in India.

A member of my Platoon had a pet monkey which somehow managed to get free. At the time a Company was on the Parade Ground carrying out a Drill Parade. The monkey, after a quick look at the Parade, dashed forward and proceeded to climb up the leg of a tall, young Officer who was, of course, wearing a kilt.

One night when I was Orderly Officer, I 'turned out the Guard'. I said to the sentry, 'If I had not stopped when you challenged me, what would you have done?'

He replied, 'I should have challenged you in Urdu.'

'Correct,' I replied, 'but what would you have said?'

The answer, again correct, was *'Kaun hai hillo mat'* ('Who's there, don't move'). I told him that he would have done the right thing and issued the right challenge. I added, 'What does *Kaun hai hillo mat* mean?' and got an answer I did not expect. It was, 'Sir, I haven't the foggiest idea.'

What a splendid bunch they all were, and I wonder what has happened to them and how many survived the war?

Chapter 3

Gurkhas

I soon learnt the status of a Gurkha Officer or an Indian Officer in an Indian Regiments. The Officers of the Indian Army were classified as King's Commissioned, regardless of nationality, or Viceroy's Commissioned Officers. The latter had many years service in their Regiment, were promoted to Officer rank after they had passed various tests, etc. They lived in the 'Lines' and were not members of the Regimental Mess. They commanded Platoons or the equivalent and the Senior G.O.s (as they were referred to) were usually second-in-command of their Companies and wore Subhedars (two pips). There were also three other major appointments: Subhedar Major, who wore a crown on his shoulder, Jemedar Adjutant (one pip), and Jemedar Quartermaster (one pip). The old ranks were Lance Naik (Lance Corporal), Naik (Corporal), Havildar (Sargeant), Havildar Major (C.S.M. or R.S.M.), Quartermaster Havildar (Q.M.S.). In fact, the duties in a Company or the Battalion were the same within the whole United Kingdom and Empire Armies, only the name was different.

Because of our G.O.s, the establishment of British Officers was about half that of a British Regiment. This often meant that, during the hot weather or leave season, numbers were very low. There were further demands for Junior Staff appointments which had to be filled. We therefore found that we Juniors had responsibilities far beyond our rank and experience. A new terminology was soon known to me, namely Company Commander Sub Protem (C.C.S.P.T.): this meant that when commanding a Company one drew an allowance for a Charger and also received a Syce's pay and allowance, which was paid out on pay day.

When I had been in the Battalion for about two days the C.O. sent for me and told me to take over as 'C' Company Commander. The C.O. added that a Senior Major would soon be back from home leave and would keep an eye on me and help when I found things difficult, and so would everyone else so long as I asked.

I went along to 'C' Company office and met Subhedar Dhanbahadur Mal, who was acting as Senior G.O. during the absence of Subhedar Bombahadur Gurung, who was on leave after Recruiting Duties.

Dhanbahadur became a great friend and went out of his way to help and advise me during the many months in the future when he was to be my Senior G.O. He was at one time Bugle Major and knew what being smart meant.

I am often asked about life in a Gurkha Regiment in the pre-war days and such questions as, 'How many Battalions were there?', etc., so I feel that I should diverge a little and give a short answer to such questions.

There were ten Regiments, numbered from 1–10, each consisting of two Battalions. It was customary to refer to them as 1/2nd and 2/2nd, etc., meaning 1st or 2nd Battalion of such and such a Regiment. The example I have given would have meant 1st Battalion 2nd Goorkhas or 2nd Battalion 2nd Goorkhas or more officially 2nd Gurkha Rifles. We used the old name. A Battalion was organised on exactly the same basis as a British Battalion, less the Indian Platoon to look after the Machine Gun Mules.

The 1st, 2nd, 3rd, 4th, 5th, 6th and 8th Gurkha Rifles enlisted tribes known as Magars and Gurungs and those connected with them. The 9th Gurkha Rifles enlisted a higher caste, namely Chettries and Takurs, and the 7th and 10th Gurkha Rifles recruited Limbus and Rais from Eastern Nepal. All Regiments had a few men from tribes or castes other than their majority intake. It made no difference whatsoever. During the war, we had some men who should have been in either the 7th or 10th Gurkha Rifles, and some of their 'close clansmen' who I had never heard of. They spoke a language of their own, were just as nice and gallant as any other Gurkha. I had a Batman in Burma who was a Tamang and he spent much of his time teaching me new words and getting a great amount of amusement as a result. The Sherpas come from Eastern Nepal, but were not a member of the regular recruited tribes.

Each Battalion trained its own recruits, who spent about a year in Training Company. There were two Recruiting Depots, one at Gorakpur for Magars, Gurungs and their 'septs', the other much further east at Gum for Limbus, Rais and their 'septs'. Each Battalion made up its own Recruiting Party, who were based on the Recruiting Depot concerned and where the Recruiting Staff, consisting of Regimental British and Gurkha Officers, remained. In those days

British Officers were not allowed into Nepal except for a specific task and only by invitation and if accompanied by their wives. The recruiting season covered only a part of the year as it was quite impossible to reach some of the places during the monsoon. There were no bridges or those that existed were washed away and the rivers were fast and deep. Our nearest recruit came from a place which was a ten-day march from the border. In addition to our Nepalese recruits, we were also allowed to enlist some of the sons and grandsons of ex-Gurkha soldiers who had settled in India, normally in a village close to their old Regimental Lines. These were known as 'Line Boys' and many rose to high rank.

At the time both 2 G.R. Battalions were in Dehra Dun, separated by about one mile of open ground which belonged to the Regiment and where we could play football and polo and also where athletics were held. It was also the venue for special parades such as Delhi Day in September of each year when the Regiment's recruits were sworn in on the Truncheon.

A Rifle Regiment, according to Army custom, did not carry colours. However, after the fall of Delhi in the Indian Mutiny the Regiment was given a special honour by Her Majesty Queen Victoria. It was a 'Truncheon' which was held and treated as a colour. The Senior Battalion, i.e. 1/2 G.R., housed the Truncheon in their Guardroom when they were stationed at Dehra Dun. If they were away for any length of time or on active service, the 2/2 G.R. looked after the Truncheon. If both Battalions were away, it was the responsibility of the Depot.

Another honour gained by ourselves, the 60th Rifles and the Guides, was that we wore a thin red band around the collar of our patrol jackets and in the case of the Guides and ourselves also on our khaki jackets. We tried to model ourselves on the 60th Rifles regarding drill, uniform, etc.; in fact we were the only Gurkha Regiment not to have bagpipes, instead we maintained a high standard of bugling. Our buglers carried and used silver bugles. It was our custom, on promotion from Lieutenant to Captain, to present a silver bugle to the Regiment — I presume mine is still in use. Another of our customs was we did not wear any badges of rank on our mess kit.

At the time I joined the 2/2 G.R. each battalion had three Subalterns. Both Battalions shared the same mess and we were all justifiably proud of it. As a result we all became very good friends and I cannot remember anyone uttering a derogatory remark about the other Battalion. We were all Officers of the 2nd Goorkhas and proud of it.

During November, 1930 we were under orders to carry out a Flag March with the 9th G.R. It had been decided that both Battalions should carry out the same route, but in opposite directions. The Civil Administration considered that riots in support of Mahatma Gandhi might break out and that it would be a good idea to show the flag. During the days before we set forth the Field Mess had to be checked, a task for the two Junior Subalterns! Companies practised pitching tents and one or two route marches were carried out.

The 9th G.R. set forth in an anti-clockwise direction and we in a clock-wise direction which meant that we started off through the wonderful jungle of the Doon. Both Battalions were to meet and camp outside a small Indian town where inhabitants included a number of young hot-heads and political agitators. Our first day's march was about seventeen miles to a forest bungalow called Lachiewala on the river Song. Here we bivouacked for the night, using the bungalow as a mess and bedroom for the C.O. The next day we followed the District Board Road through the jungle to the forest bungalow and camping ground at Raiwala, which was on high ground overlooking the river Ganges. Here we lived in tents and we remained for a number of days.

While at Raiwala it was decided that we Officers should go up to Rikkikesh in the Mess car. The Ganges made its exit from the Himalayas at this place and was the centre for Hindus (and others) who were making a pilgrimage to Badrinath, the source of the river Ganges. The river in this area was holy to many, so we were careful not to cause any offence or enter any building. People were very pleasant and we received many smiles and, of course, questions as to who we were and what we were doing there.

While we were standing on a bridge across the Ganges looking at some large fish we were surprised to hear an English voice say, 'Good afternoon, can I help you?' We turned round and found an Englishman dressed as a Sadu, who told us that he had been an Officer in a Yorkshire Regiment and that his name was Captain Young. He added that his present name was Ghahananun, which roughly translated means 'chosen of God'. He invited us to cross the river and have a mug of tea with him at the 'cults' camp and meet some of the others. The first people we met were a young couple. She was South African and he, I think, Australian.

I heard later that the Police had told them to move elsewhere.

While we enjoyed a mug of tea, the Head of the community arrived. He, during his working days, had been a Judge in Southern India. He proved to be a most charming and educated man and was, I think, a Hindu of high caste in origin. But, as he explained, a true Sadu is really above religion, in that he believes in one God of all religions, and that all human beings belong to him. All can become Sadus if they merit the honour. He explained in simple language why Hindus had so many Gods represented by statues, all very sensible and understandable when explained by such a man as the Judge. He and Young told us that the ordinary people would give food and money to anyone dressed in saffron clothes, as he might be a Sadu. Neither of our new friends were ever short of anything they required.

Because of this we had to beware of rogues and charlatans and of many of those who appeared to be ascetics. We asked the Judge and Young to visit us in our camp the next evening as our band and bugles were Beating Retreat and to bring some others with them. Before leaving these kind folk, we were taken to see a new Hindu temple which was being built. The design was explained to us and, after we had removed our shoes, we were taken inside and introduced to the temple staff.

As we were leaving for camp the Judge said, 'I know that you will want to shoot and fish. Do so by all means, but we should prefer that you carry out such activities about four miles from this place.'

The next evening our friends watched Retreat and then came into the Mess for a glass of orange squash.

A day or so after our meeting with the community, we were shooting in an area not far from our camp. While walking along a dry Nullah (water course), I shot a peacock, which fell round a bend in the Nullah bed. When we rounded the bend we found that the bird had dropped between us and a small Hindu temple. I wondered what the outcome might be, as to most Hindus the peacock is sacred, but not to a Gurkha of my regiment. Subhedar Dhanbahadur ordered one of the beaters ('C' Company) to put the bird into a sack and carry on with their beating. To my horror I saw a Hindu priest walking towards us. He approached and said that he would be very pleased if I would accept a basket of sweet limes. I thanked him very much for his gift and accepted with pleasure.

I left with his blessing and smiles all round. I recount this incident to try and show that we can all be friendly, understanding and tolerant of one another no matter what faith we follow. I was starting to learn the truth of the saying, 'There are no bad religions, it is the abuses of religion which are bad'. To this I would add also ignorance. I was to learn more during the war.

We marched about fifteen miles per day to the next camp, but our next march was a short one to a place called Hardwar, where there was a camping ground and some excellent bungalows belonging to the Public Works Department (P.W.D.) and their officers for the maintenance of the dam which was just upstream. Close to our Mess there was a large tank looked after by Hindu priests. The tank contained a large number of sacred fish. Pilgrims gained merit by buying food and feeding the Mahseer. I bought some food, which I held in my fingers, on instruction of a priest I put my hand in the water and the fish took the food from my hand.

Below the dam we could see many fish, including gigantic Goonch. I was amused by the Goonch, they just lay there, opened their large mouths and caught the small fish, that were washed over the dam or failed to find the fish pass.

Our Second-in-Command joined us at Hardwar. He was to be our next Commanding Officer. He had been on home leave and lived at Fleet. He sponsored me for the Regiment, had told me to apply to be attached to the Black Watch, so that the Regiment could 'vet' me (I was delighted with the thought of being attached to a Highland Regiment). He brought with him my parents' twenty-first birthday present which I am wearing now.

We had been given permission to march along the banks of the Ganges canal on a first-class road. It was the habit of most Regiments to start their marches early in the morning and to halt at some convenient place approximately half-way along the route. We called this 'Half Road' and the Q.M. and this staff used to precede the Battalion, often the night before, and would lay on a meal. By the time we reached 'Half Road' I was ready for a large meal — and got it! Our march continued. At one place, I cannot remember the name, we had a little trouble from a young man who thought it was a good opportunity to spread some anti-British propaganda amongst the troops. The C.O. had taken the British and Gurkha Officers out on reconnaissance a short distance from canal to allocate Company Training areas, leaving the M.G. Company and their Company Commander in camp to carry on with M.G. training. When we got back we heard a lot of laughter and saw a dripping young man.

We learnt that he had approached some men of the M.G. Company and had attempted to spread his propaganda.

The men were furious and flung him into the canal where he was rapidly washed downstream. His antics and struggles amused the men, who pulled him out, took him upstream and flung him in again. The trouble was the youth could not swim. There was a lot of trouble for the Company Commander from the Civil Authorities. However, it was all cleared up and no-one except the hot-headed youth was any the worse.

After spending a varying amount of days training at various camps, we met the 9th G.R. at a camp where we spent about four days. This halt was at the request of Civil Authority and the camping area was close to a small Indian town which housed a number of trouble makers. It was here that I was to learn that the Gurhka, with all his charm and tremendous sense of humour, also has a quick temper.

The 9th G.R. Pipes and Drums and our Regimental Band and Bugles had just finished Beating a Combined Retreat, when a young hot-head threw a hockey stick at the Bands. The Regimental Police, who had been 'Keeping the Ground', spotted the young man and escorted him into our lines. What they did to the young man I did not witness, but there were many loud yells. When the youth was set free he ran off into the 9th G.R. Lines, where there were more yells. I was told later that the youth had had various portions of his anatomy threatened with a sharp kukri. Apart from a bad fright, the youth was not hurt in any way and we had no more trouble during our stay in that area.

We had a lot of entertainment from numerous villages and their councils. This normally took the form of a tea party where we met the village elders. At the entrance to most villages through which we marched arches had been built connected by red banners either saying 'Welcome' or 'Long Live King George'. On one occasion we were greeted by the village band playing 'God Save the King'.

Anyone who has heard an Indian village band will know the sort of noise it makes. When added to the strains of a Regimental Band blowing their hardest, the noise is incredible. The villagers of India are nice people and most generous to strangers. They are seldom out of debt, which more than likely was originated by their father or grandfather, and the moneylenders make certain that the interest can never be paid off.

The two Battalions continued with the march and a few days later I was sent back to Dehra Dun suffering from a bad dose of 'Doon tummy'. This illness was no different from any other 'bad tummy', each area in India claimed it under its own name!

When I got back to Dehra Doon I went to my quarters in bungalow no. 13 called Orange Lodge. In those days we owned all the bungalows in Catonments and very pretty and cool they were, with their thatched roofs and well-kept gardens. However, there came a time when we were forced to sell them to the Army Authorities and they became Army Quarters.

I had only been in my quarter a very short time when the Second-in-Command's wife came in to see me and to tell me that an M.O. had been sent for and would be here soon. This lady was very kind and took great care of me. I was soon up and about and had my meals with my kind friend.

As soon as I was allowed to, and was declared fit, I went up to the office and met Subhedar Bombahadur Gurung, who had returned from leave. Subhedar Bombahadur was a great character with a first-class war record and many medals on his chest.

He gave me a good look over and said, 'You, Sahib know nothing about commanding a Company of Gurkhas. I shall tell you what to do and teach you.'

He was, of course, quite right and I was very impressed by his soldierly bearing and turnout.

Under Bombahadur's eagle eye I learnt a lot, including how to use a 'kukri'. He gave me a well-balanced kukri and eventually he said, 'Now you are ready to behead a goat!'.

I had to do it and the Company enjoyed goat as a meal. The next Dusserah, one of the men, came up to where we Officers and G.O.s were sitting and handed me a sacrificial kukri and demanded that I should sacrifice a goat. I carried out the sacrifice and luckily my aim was true — I had been well taught.

In the Christmas draw for 'Forest Blocks' for Christmas shoots the Regiment had been lucky. The C.O. of the 1st Battalion had drawn a good Block on the south side of the Siwalik Hills. He said he would visit the Block in the hopes of shooting a tiger or panther.

He gave the Block to a Subaltern in the 1st Battalion and myself provided we looked after an R.A.F. friend of his. The Wing Commander was a good companion and we very much enjoyed our Christmas.

I became firm friends with the cow elephant we had with us. She was a most intelligent animal, gentle and altogether delightful.

After Christmas we went back to Dehra Dun and prepared for the Proclamation Parade, which took place on the 1st of January each year. The whole Brigade took part in the parade which was in honour of Queen Victoria's nomination as Empress of India. The parade took place on our main polo ground, so we did not have to move very far.

Chapter 4

Regimental Duties and Leisure

Life as a young Regimental Office in pre-war India included many and varied duties, as well as considerable hours of leisure. Queen Victoria had declared that the Army in India should have one complete day off a week. For most of the Army of the period of which I now record, the selected day was Thursday. The Regiments in Dehra Dun had chosen Saturdays as their 'day off'. This had many advantages and before long was adopted by, I think, the whole Army.

We always had to be prepared for two emergencies, communal riots and trouble breaking out on the North-West Frontier. We were often called out at Company strength to wait, in the Bazaar, for trouble to break out. In other words, we were acting in aid of the Civil Power, or in a wider sense were carrying out 'imperial policing'. I spent several hours carrying out these duties, but never once experienced anything in the nature of a riot.

Frontier warfare had to be practised at regular periods and usually took the form of a T.E.W.T. (Tactical Exercise Without Troops). These normally took place on some convenient ground, shaped like hills, before breakfast. By the time they were over we were all ready for something to eat!

During this period of preliminary training, each man had an opportunity to carry out firing on the ranges and to attend a company or two-company week or ten days at Field Firing Camp, about ten miles from our Lines.

The men enjoyed these camps and so did the Officers. The river Suswa ran close by and contained a number of small fish, which the men caught. There was also good shooting in the area. The open season for game birds seldom coincided with camp, but hares abounded.

21

The Gurkha considered the hare as one of the most desirable of meals. It was said that a severe test of discipline was to let a hare loose during a Ceremonial Parade and see how many men broke ranks.

I remember one shoot very well. We were walking across an area with the beaters in line. The 'Guns' were the Company Commander of 'B' Company, myself and G.O.s who had guns. A hare got up and ran off. I missed it with both barrels. However, either my Orderly or another beater, drew his kukri and threw it at the animal, muttering as he did so that he did not think much of the markmanship. He hit the hare on the back of the neck and had hare for the evening meal!

We had plenty to do in our spare time. There was football, with a Battalion team to train for the Gurkha Brigade Cup, polo three times a week, golf on our own golf course, athletics, several gymkhanas, Saturday evening dances at the club and always some hope of fishing or shooting at weekends. The Doon and other Indian jungles had a very special appeal to me. The big Hindu festivals were much loved by the men, as there were a number of 'Khanas' (evening feasts) to which the British Officers were invited. These Khanas taught us, who required it, to speak the Gurkhas' language. Some British Officers spoke Nepali very well and knew a lot about the Gurkha.

All young Officers of the Indian Army were required to pass two examinations: a language examination, either at lower or higher standard, and the Retention examination. When the time came for me to take the Retention examination, which consisted of drill, weapon training, map reading and Regimental history, I presented myself at Birpur to face a board of 9th G.R. Officers under the chairmanship of the C.O. (nine years later he became my father-in-law). He failed me in drill — quite rightly so. The next time I was tested I passed.

In 1932 I was sent on a Regimental Officers' Signals Course at Poona. At Poona I played a lot of cricket and kept wicket for the Gymkhana Club on several occasions. An excellent club at Poona was the Race Club. I could not afford to join two clubs, nor could my friend in the Cameronians. So we joined one each and took each other to the one we had joined, as a guest.

The racing on Saturdays was great fun, but neither my friend nor I became millionaires. We took a little money with us to the meetings we attended and when that was finished we called it a day and went to the club I had joined and celebrated our losses.

During the course the monsoon broke, so we managed to play quite a lot of rugger. It was suggested, that during the long mid-course break, we would challenge the Bombay team. This we did and our challenge was accepted.

Bombay, Calcutta and Madras had first-class teams. We were advertised in Bombay as a Combined Services XV.

The game was a good one and we lost, but only by a very small margin. After the game we were taken by our opponents to the Bombay Gymkhana club, which had one of the longest bars in the old Empire! Their system was to start with a collection of club members who were having a drink and to say, 'Playing rugger down here'. Our hosts then left for the far end of the bar, which we eventually reached having been passed from one group of members to another. Our rugby hosts 'caught' us and gave us a meal!

Someone at the bar stated that it would be a good idea if the two teams played each other at soccer that night. It was soon arranged and decided that the kick-off should be at midnight and the ground the open space in front of the "Gateway of India". Only one set of goal posts would be necessary and that would be the Gateway. The ball had to be a coconut, rules did not matter.

We kicked-off and spent a wonderful time behaving like children until the police turned up and a British Police Sergeant said that enough was enough. I was returned to an hotel sitting on the bonnet of a police car. The party continued for a short time. I then returned to the Headquarters Mess of the Royal Indian Marine.

Before leaving Poona for the match, I had written to the Mess Secretary to ask if my Cameronian friend and I could stay in their Mess during our time in Bombay. We had a most kind reply and were extremely well looked after. I met many R.I.M. Officers, some of whom knew my father. Some showed us Bombay, all were excellent hosts.

I managed to pass the course and returned to the Battalion, who had moved from Dehra Dun to the Malakand on the North-West Frontier of India.

Needless to say after my Signal course and visit to Bombay I was broke, so much so in fact, that I refused the kind invitation of a Gunner to spend the night at Nowshera in the R.A. Mess. I did not think that I could afford a Mess bill, so I spent the night in the waiting room at the railway station and caught the train to Dargai the next morning.

On my return to the Battalion I found myself commanding 'C' Company, and as Signal Officer. Bombahadur had gone on pension and Sub. Dhanbahadur Mal was again my senior G.O.

The Malakand was across the main road from Peshawar and Nowshera through Rissalpur and Mardan to Swat and Dir, two independent states run respectively by their rulers the Wali of Swat and the Nawab of Dir. I had the pleasure of visiting Dir to shoot, and met the Wali's son. Malakand was one of the few frontier stations where Officers' wives were allowed.

The main fort, the Malakand, was built on a ridge overlooking the main road and the exit to a tunnel which allowed the Swat canal to flow down to the plains. The Fort held at least a Battalion of Infantry and a Station Staff Officer, the Political Agent and small staff. There was an excellent library run by the wives. On a hill above the Fort was a Block House manned by a Platoon and some Battalion Signallers, For recreation there was a full-sized football ground, used also for polo, and excellent Chickoor and See See shooting. The P.A. had the sole right to fish a portion of the river Swat, which was fished by us on invitation, but it was necessary to be escorted by a Levy Guard.

There were two detached forts, Dargai at Railhead and Chakdara on the right bank of the river Swat, about twelve miles from the Malakand on the Dir side of the river, which was crossed by a bridge guarded on the Swat side (left) by a Levy Guard who was responsible for closing the bridge at 'Stand To'.

The river Swat ran under the fort walls and held some good-sized fish — Mahseer, Chirroo and Chush. The fields across the bridge on the Swat side had plenty of duck, snipe, green plover and other game at the right season, also a few woodcock.

The fort could hold a Battalion but was normally held by a Company of Infantry and a Troop of 4.5 Howitzers manned by Indian Gunners. Chakdara always reminded me of something out of a novel by P. C. Wren. A block house stood on a steep hill, above the fort and was manned by a Section of Infantry and Battalion Signallers. Communication was maintained with the Malakand through this Piquet by heliograph during the day and lamp at night. The Piquet was called Signal Piquet, but was in fact, Ghunga Din's Piquet in the well-known poem by Rudyard Kipling.

There was, of course, a telephone link with Battalion headquarters. An excellent account of the old battles to conquer Malakand and Chakdara is given in Sir Winston Churchill's book *The Malakand Field Force*.

I loved my time at Chakdara. Few Officers of my age and service found themselves twelve miles from Headquarters and 'Supreme Commander' of a fort. If I had not quite finished my letter to my parents I would send word to the Post Master, who instructed the post van to wait — I never heard of the mail train to Bombay being late!

There were good training areas close to Chakdara, also a 600-yard range and sport grounds covered in grass.

The men also liked the fort. They could bathe in the river and catch small fish in their nets.

I spent a tour of duty at Dargai, and it was there that I met the next Subaltern to join. After he had had some breakfast the mess car from Malakand took him up the hill where I next met him.

Regimental life went on with breaks to classify the Guides Signallers at Mardan, and a visit to our 1st Battalion who had moved to the Khyber Pass and were stationed at Jamrud. The C.O. of the 1st Battalion was a Scot and he had taught the mess cook to make haggis. I enjoyed haggis for the first dinner we had at Jamrud. I had to put up with the usual remarks made by my English and Irish brother Officers. However, I maintain that they enjoyed their dinner in spite of their Sassenach remarks!. We also spent a fortnight in Red Shirt Country, which made a change of scene and showed the Flag.

I found it difficult to pass the Urdu examination for two reasons. I wanted to learn the language of our men and I did not work as I should have done.

I was, however, able to obtain a vacancy on a language course run by Army Headquarters at Simla. It was an excellent course and taught a lot of other things apart from the language, such as religious beliefs and Indian customs. At the end of the course I passed the higher standard Urdu with ease and could read and write the Nagri script. Without being able to read and write in the appropriate script it was very difficult to master the correct pronunciation in Urdu and Nepali. When I left Simla, I wondered why such a course had not been compulsory for U.L.I.A. Officers.

On arrival back at the Battalion I learnt that the next year I should attend a weapon training course at the Small Arms School, Pachmarhi, after which I could apply for home leave.

Pachmarhi was a semi-hill station in the Mahdeo Hills in the Central Indian Province.

The Malakand attracted large numbers of visitors as it was a reasonably safe place to be and visit. The local tribesmen were friendly and very pleased to sell their wares and farm produce to the Garrison. But not far away were other tribes, such as Mohmands, so all gates were shut and locked at dusk. Neither did we use the road to Dargai or Chakdara after dusk. The Political Agent kept us informed of the situation. One Political Agent, who we all liked very much, was shot and killed while at the head of a column in the Mohmand country during our time in Malakand.

Two visits remain in my memory. One was from an Admiral and his staff. The Admiral was a V.C. holder from the Great War and lived near to my family home. I had never met him but knew his house and some of his wife's family, who also came from Moray. The Admiral and his staff were most welcome guests and he told me many years later, when I met him in Moray, that he too had enjoyed his visit to the Malakand.

Another lot of visitors we had was a Parliamentary Delegation who had been badly briefed before leaving England and knew very little about India in general and the Frontier in particular. I suppose that their main reason for the visit was to learn something — I hope they did! I recall their surprise when we took them for a walk outside the Fort and they saw the local people working their fields with rifles slung over their shoulders. We told them that there was little danger as Pathans carried rifles for their own protection in the Malakand against any chance of a blood-feud taking them unawares. I hope that they believed us.

This visit came on a day when I had taken 'C' Company out to a hill to practise establishing a Piquet on the top of the hill. Any sensible British Officer would not attempt to keep up with Gurkhas coming away from a hill at speed. I did, and learnt a lesson!

While I was going at speed trying to keep up with a wave of men, and I was jumping from rock to rock, I saw a snake lying on some grass where I intended to land. I broke an Olympic record or two by hardly touching land before I jumped again. On landing Sub. Dhanbahadour seized me and started to remove one of my ankle puttees. I asked him what was wrong and he replied that, as quick as I was, the snake was even quicker. It had whipped round and struck me just above my right ankle but had not penetrated the puttee. My orderly drew his sword (bayonet) and killed the snake which was said to be a viper, or it may have been a krite.

I continued my journey down-hill and must have fallen as I came to on the road.

Before leaving for Pachmarhi I had one more tour of duty at Chakdara. A bridge over a river in Dir, at a place called Ballinbat, had been washed away and the Sappers repairing the bridge required protecting. A small Column was sent up with the Sappers, as escort, from the Abbotabad Brigade.

I met a number of Officers in the 5th Royal Gurkha Rifles and 6th Gurkha Rifles. One of which was to be a valued friend under whom I served both in Burma and later in India.

The river Swat was the boundary between war and peace, so Chakdara was considered to be in the operational zone. We all drew operational rations, which included cigarettes and/or tobacco. The fort filled up with other troops including armoured cars and I soon commanded quite a garrison. The building of a new bridge took about three weeks and we were soon back to normal routine.

One afternoon the Political Agent and I had a walk over the fields for an hour or so. On our return to Chakdara, where the P.A. had kindly offered to drop me, we had to cross the bridge. The Levy Sentry failed to recognise the P.A.'s car and failed to turn out the Guard. The P.A. was furious and shouted for the Havildar of the Guard, who arrived and turned several shades lighter. When he could get a word in he said, 'Sir, may I speak to you?'

The reply he got, and the majestic way in which it was said, was to me, quite amusing: 'You may look at me, you may admire me from afar, but you may not speak to me!'

I went to Pachmarhi on the Small Arms Course and passed it. One afternoon when we were changing out of uniform the earth shook and our quarters swayed about. Several cars shook like jellies and we had to wait until all was over. We knew what it was — an earthquake, but we did not know where it was or what damage it had caused until later. It was, what was termed, the First Behar Earthquake and it caused a lot of damage and loss of life. It had taken place many miles from Pachmarhi but we all felt the severe shock.

After the course I caught a train for Bombay and went aboard the P. & O. ship *Maloja* for eight months' home leave.

I had arranged to meet my old Regimental friend in Paris, as he had decided to take short home leave. However, this did not take place as my friend developed severe eye trouble and was put into hospital at Malta. At Malta I had an Uncle and Aunt. He was in the R.N. and they looked after my friend.

On my friend's arrival in England we spent many good days in London and I had the added pleasure of staying a few days at his home in Dorset and meeting his charming parents.

While in Dorset we played a lot of golf and had a day's partridge shooting as the guests of the local Member of Parliament.

My parents had moved to the Channel Islands and on that leave I was unable to visit Scotland, which was a great disappointment to me as before leaving India that was one of the things I most wanted to do.

Chapter 5

Life at Pachmarhi

During my home leave I heard that I had been selected as an Instructor on the Indian wing Small Arms School, Pachmarhi. Later I heard that A.H.Q. India considered that I might like to attend a Weapon Training Conference at Hythe. I accepted with pleasure, although it meant giving up some of my leave. I said farewell to my parents, as it was not worth returning to the Channel Islands for a few days. The Hythe Conference was most instructive as several new weapons were demonstrated. I was the only Indian Army Officer to attend the conference. I think I was looked upon as a curio! The weather was cold and there was a bitter wind from the East for the whole of the three days at Hythe.

I was delighted to have a large fire in my room each night. The cost of the coal was charged as an item on my Mess bill. When I got back to India I was instructed to claim 'Expenses'. The only item to be disallowed was the coal, on the grounds that Indian Army Officers did not get free coal. I did not argue the claim, just accepted some Pay Babu's interpretation of regulations!

Life at Pachmarhi was most pleasant and the work both interesting and instructive, as every caste and class of soldier of the Army in India attended Weapons Courses. All Officers attended the British wing. Students included men from Burma, Indian State Forces and men from semi-military Forces.

There was plenty to do for leisure, as at the Small Arms School there were both hockey and football grounds. There was also a cricket ground, golf course and tennis courts which were included in club membership. In the jungle there was shooting, both big game and small. During the winter, panther became quite bold and were seen close to our bungalows. During my time at Pachmarhi at least one tiger spent a night or two on the golf course. The small game shooting was in the jungle, at the foot of the hill road to Pachmarhi. The jungle fowl were different to those in the Dehra Dun area, which were the red jungle fowl and looked just like domestic bantams. These jungle fowl had feathers which looked as if they had been dipped in varnish and because of their general colouring were known as grey jungle fowl. There were also spur fowl, so named due to the fact that the cocks had two spurs on each leg. Other birds such as peafowl, duck, snipe and some sand grouse, also grey and black partridge and quail lived in the area.

The hill road to Pachmarhi entered the plains at a place called Singanama which had an excellent rest house.

Singanama was on a tributary of the river Narbada where there were some fish to be caught. Big game such as tiger, panther, sloth and black bear, also various types of deer and many varieties of wild cat and pig lived in these jungles. I was lucky enough to see most varieties and was always astounded by the beauty of a beast in the wilds. I was not very interested in shooting big game, watching them gave me all the thrill I needed. I did, however, enjoy small game shooting, they were a welcome change of diet and very good to eat.

As all of our work took place out of doors it was impossible to do anything in the way of weapon training during the monsoon so the School closed for a period of four months, when it rained non-stop. Those who could, often took short leave to the U.K. I did in 1936 as it was not my turn to supervise the Cavalry that year. I had also had two attacks of malaria followed by jaundice so I thought it would be a good idea to have a period of home air and food. I spent a grand leave in Scotland, in Elgin, shot my first grouse and grassed my first salmon. People who owned any shooting or fishing in pre-war days were very generous to young Officers like myself and invitations poured in. I also heard that I had passed my promotion examination to Captain.

During my leave I heard from Joan Burnett, whose mother had died the previous year. She told me that old family friends were moving up to Pachmarhi in September, which was part of the twice-yearly move for members of the C.P. Civil Administration. She added that she was now able to leave her father and sister and that her friends had said that they would chaperone her. I wrote back to the Indian Military Academy, Dehra Dun, where Joan's father was Assistant Commandant, asking Joan to please accept her friends' invitation. I knew Joan's friends well and had been at Sandhurst with their son. I had been back in Pachmarhi for a day or so when Joan and I became engaged.

After the necessary permission to be married had been received, we fixed a date for 8th March, 1937, which fell in the interval between two courses.

I left Pachmarhi for Dehra Dun on 5th March, 1937, after a party at the club given by my friends at the Small Arms School. We were married on 8th March, 1937, and after the reception we left for our honeymoon, of only a few days, at the rest house at Fathepur and fishing in the river Arsan. My new father-in-law lent us his large V8 for our honeymoon so we were able to see some of the country, which included a trip up to Saiha.

On our return to Pachmarhi we lived at the Pachmarhi Hotel in a small quarter. After a few weeks we were able to transfer to a larger bungalow. During the monsoon we discovered the Pachmarhi mushrooms, which grew in their hundreds on the Plateau if you knew where to look for them.

By this time we had acquired a car from one of the Instructors whose tenure had come to an end. After twenty-nine days of non-stop rain we decided that we would motor up to Dehra Dun and visit the family, a distance of over 650 miles in the Monsoon. Of course we were mad! We had a number of rivers to cross by bridge or ferry, but we were young and we carried extra petrol, tyres, etc. My Bearer, Sher Singh had also had a short course and knew how to change a tyre. One of the great snags, of motoring in India, was the menace of broken bullock shoes. The bullock cart was the normal vehicle used by Indians as transport for everything. The bullocks were shod and the shoes either broke or came off and were left on the roads as sharp pieces of metal. The front wheels of a car would throw them towards the back wheels and they then penetrated the tyre and inner tube, thus causing a blow out or at least a puncture. The only answer was to have flaps fitted and even these did not always prevent damage to the tyres.

Our route took us through Jubbulpore, Jhansi, Gwalior, Agra, Delhi and Meerut. We spent the first night at a rest house somewhere on the route and the second night at the club in Agra.

Just south of Jhansi is the river Betwa, which in the monsoon is a raging torrent. In normal times there is a 'bridge of boats' across the river, but in the monsoon the bridge is replaced by a ferry. We found notices diverting us to the ferry via a second-class sandy road. We were motoring down the road when we met two very large bulls the one at the back suddenly butted his pal in the front, who swung his head round and one of his very fine horns went through our windscreen. There was nothing we could do about it so we carried on towards the ferry, which was approached by about seventy-five yards of sand and we soon became stuck. However, this was normal procedure and wonderful to relate, willing helpers appeared from the Heavens and soon had us out of the sand for the cost of a few annas.

We crossed the river on the ferry and reached Agra where we managed to find a room for the night and have a good dinner. During the evening the clouds broke up and the sky cleared so we decided to motor out to the Taj Mahal, it was quite magnificent. I had heard so much about the Taj that I was quite prepared to be disappointed. Nothing could have been further from my mind and I was astounded by its beauty and the great sense of peace that one had looking at it. We were glad that we were the only visitors present.

We reached Dehra Dun after a hot, dusty but excellent journey with no further argument with bulls.

After an excellent holiday, Joan's sister said that she would like to accept our invitation and spend a few weeks with us.

I had a new windscreen fitted at the garage at Dehra Dun and had submitted a claim to the insurance company. Between Delhi and Agra, the road ran beneath some large trees whose branches often met in the middle of the road. A lot of monkeys were chasing each other in the trees, when suddenly a young one missed the branch and fell on to the bonnet of our car up against the new windscreen! Luckily no damage was done but I wondered what the insurance company would have thought if I had had to claim. On the way up a bull put its horn through the windscreen, on the way back a monkey fell through the windscreen!

One other memory comes back as I think of this journey. During the monsoon every bug hatches out and about two million were on the wall of our bedroom at Agra. Only the lizards enjoyed them and they could hardly move as they had eaten so many. I do not think that Joan enjoyed the situation very much, but we were under a mosquito net so felt reasonably safe from attack!

We crossed the river Betwa on the ferry which, because of the strong current, ended up several hundred yards from where we were intended to land. However, there were soon plenty of men to tow us upstream. It was during this crossing that I saw two things of note. The first was a very large fish which jumped out of the water. I did not see it for long but to me it looked like a dolphin. The second was, I saw the largest crocodile I ever saw in India. It slithered down the river bank into the water.

The rest of the journey was quite normal and our car behaved well.

Back in Pachmarhi we played golf, bathed at the swimming pool, Bea Dam, and showed Joan's sister the country round Pachmarhi and took our two dogs for walks.

Just below Pachmarhi on the road to Singanama was a cultivated plateau whose name I cannot remember. On this plateau were some old caves, said to contain ancient treasure. A retired Gunner Major and his wife came to our hotel, where they made their base, for treasure hunting.

We often spoke to them and heard what they hoped to find. Alas it was not to be, the Major developed a disease, which I think was typhus, and died. We attended his funeral and did what we could for his wife who soon left Pachmarhi and moved somewhere in India.

The large Pachmarhi plateau was dominated by two hills sacred to Hindus. The largest and steepest was Mahdeo and the smaller, much more accessible was Dhup Ghar. We climbed both these hills. The summit of Mahdeo was reached by a flight of stone steps. I estimated that there were about 200 steep steps — I did the climb once only and Joan stayed at the bottom of the stairway with the other wives who prepared our picnic. At the summit was a small temple looked after by a Hindu Priest to whom we gave a small amount of money. The path up and down contained a number of pilgrims who were friendly and wished us well.

Dhup Ghar was not nearly as sacred as Mahdeo and it was normal not to meet anyone en route to the summit or, apart from we British, anyone who bothered to go there except for some special festival. The name means 'House of the Sun' and it was somewhat similar to Stonehenge and was treated in much the same way.

We spent a lot of our weekends in the jungle or bathing at Singanama. We always returned after dark having taken every precaution to prevent mosquitos from having a meal off us and in this way saw a lot of wild animals, which thrilled both of us.

In March, 1938, my appointment as an Instructor was due to finish and we were due for Home Leave. We booked our passage on a new P & O ship, the *Stratheden* and very comfortable it was. Apart from the British athletic team returning from Australia we met several Army and other friends. We had booked to Tilbury. It had been a most enjoyable three years, especially the last year when I was a married man. Those were the days when a Marriage Allowance was not given to an Officer before he was thirty years old, so as far as the Army was concerned we were not married and, of course, Officers such as I, who were under thirty years of age, were referred to as 'living in sin'!

I was lucky as both before and after our wedding the civilians who came up for the hot weather were most generous with their invitations, including H.E. the Governor and his wife. An uncle of mine, of the same name, had been a popular Forest Officer in the Central Provinces and most of the senior civilians knew and liked him.

This uncle moved from Burma to the C.P. where he rose to the rank of Chief Conservator of Forests in the C.P.

We became friends with the Chief Conservator at that time and were lucky enough to be asked to be guests of his wife and himself at their Christmas Camp. The camp was at a place called Nanda situated some seventeen miles off the main road. The road to the camp had been made up by the local inhabitants, who were Ghonds. These delightful people were simple sons of nature, dressed mostly in a large smile, and for armament they carried a small home-made axe. They were very honest people and very brave. The local Forest Officer told me a story about these people which illustrates their honesty and simplicity. The Forest Officer, during one of his inspections, found that one of the tribe had been cutting down trees which had not been given to the Ghonds for firewood or any other purpose. The culprit soon came forward and received the established punishment of having his axe confiscated for one or two weeks. The man knew he had done wrong and had angered the Forest Officer Sahib, so he must accept the situation and both he and his family had to learn to do without the axe for a bit. The Ghonds used their axes for every purpose, as the Gurkha used his kukri. During the period of confiscation it never entered anyone's head that the culprit should borrow an axe!

After Christmas dinner the whole village were asked to come up to our camp and listen to the King Emperor's Christmas message. The Headman was given a place of honour by our hosts and hostess. Even our two elephants were present! After the 'Message' was finished our host asked the Headman how he had enjoyed it. The reply he got was, 'I did not understand one word, but it was wonderful to hear the King Emperor's voice.'

We had a truly magnificent camp which included two tiger beats run by experts, plus some shooting for the 'pot'. I shot a large python and a crocodile, both of which contributed to such items as shoes, belts, wallets, etc.

Time to return to Pachmarhi soon came and we returned for my last course as an Instructor. But I cannot resist a word about our two cow elephants.

Our host was known as an expert trainer of elephants which I was able to prove. On one tiger beat one of the 'Guns' wounded a tigress. Our host, mounted on our senior elephant, came up to the tree on which we had a machan and asked me if I had seen the wounded tigress and if so what did she look like. I had seen the tigress and, most important of all, the position of her tail which was curved. Every beater, on hearing the alarm signal on a whistle, had taken to the trees and they knew that they must stay there until our host told them it was safe to come down. After a short time we heard the elephant trumpet once, followed by a rifle shot. The wounded tigress had charged but the noble elephant had stood stock-still and our host had shot the tigress in mid-air.

This elephant once killed a wounded tiger, who charged, by picking up a tree tiger in mid-air. I have known many Indian elephants, including Bandoola, during the Burma Campaign. I also knew 'Elephant Bill' and his wife, but I have never known any who were more gentle and lovable than the one I have just described.

She could find and remove apples, bananas, etc., hidden in one's pocket and one could hardly feel her great trunk searching for titbits. It is very sad to hear of the poaching in Africa and India to obtain ivory. The two great beasts are very different and I only knew the Indian elephant. I have met and admired these gentle giants both in India and Burma and I hope that some way can be found to reduce the dreadful slaughter before it is too late and these noble beasts join the dodo.

Chapter 6

Return to the Battalion

We left Pachmarhi in March 1938 and went aboard the new P & O Liner, the *Stratheden*, at Bombay bound for what we thought was eight months' leave.

After spending a couple of months in England when we met my parents, whom Joan had met once in the Channel Islands before we became engaged, time was spent being 'looked at' by our new relations! Joan's Father and sister came back from India, he had now retired. During May we motored up to Elgin where an old friend had found us a house for most of our leave.

Before leaving for Scotland the C.O. designated to take over command of 2/2 G.R. asked me to have lunch with him in London as he wished to have a talk with me. During an excellent lunch he offered me the appointment of Adjutant of 2/2 G.R. Needless to say I was delighted.

We had a wonderful leave in Elgin and I was overjoyed to learn that Joan, like myself, had every intention of retiring to those parts. The lease on the house we had rented was up about a month before we were due to return to India. In the meantime, the world situation was looking very grave, but we thought all would be well and that we should be able to finish our leave. Kind friends asked us to stay with them for the week before we went down to my parents who were now living in Camberley.

One evening we had the pleasure of seeing the North Sea Fleet enter the Sutors of Cromarty for Invergordon. We had seen the Mediterranean Fleet leave Gibraltar on our way home.

The same night we were asked, by friends, to have supper with them at Gordonstoun, which was then a new school run by an ex-German whose brother had just got away from Germany. We had a long talk and I did not like the news he gave us.

The next morning only a cruiser and her destroyer escort were to be seen in the Moray Firth, the rest of the Fleet were at 'Action Stations'.

A day or so later my host and I were sitting on the steps of his house when the postman arrived. My host handed me a letter, which I recognised was from the C.O. The letter instructed me to return to India as soon as possible. We managed to obtain accommodation on an earlier P & O and, against strong advice, Joan said that she was coming too.

The night before we left England there was an air-raid practice alert. I had fixed up some sort of blackout with the aid of one of my mother's black petticoats but it was not good enough and I had to listen to a lecture from the Air-Raid Warden. He also told me, that it would be a wise precaution to dig a slit trench behind the flat.

I told him that the next day, I was leaving Victoria Station for France en route for India leaving my parents in the flat and that they were quite incapable of digging slit trenches. He said he would make a note of it.

We left Victoria Station on the day of the signing of the Munich Agreement not knowing what was going to happen. At Paris we found a few troop trains in the station and quite a lot of Reservists. No-one had heard any real news and it was not until we reached Marseilles the next morning that we learnt from our Agent that Munich had taken place. There were quite a number of liners in port, either homeward bound or bound for Australia, New Zealand, the Far East or India, plus a glimpse of what might have been our escort, destroyers of the British Navy.

As it can be imagined it was a very cheerful voyage to Bombay with 'No War' celebrations taking place at regular intervals.

We caught the mail train at Bombay and after a night's journey got out at some station the next morning about 9.00 a.m.

Before leaving for our leave we had lent our car to a doctor friend of ours, on condition that when he heard from us he would send the car by rail to a nominated station. This he did, but we had got to the station an hour or two before the car and thought we were stuck! The journey to Dehra Dun, where both our Battalions were stationed, was without event and we arrived in good order at our great friend's bungalow and we met his wife for the first time. Our dogs, Bee a Labrador and Gretel a Dachshund, had been staying with our friends while we were on leave and both were full of beans. These friends were about to go home on leave but had to wait until he handed over the duties of

Adjutant to me. We remained as guests of our two kind friends for about a week, before moving into our own bungalow.

The new C.O. did not agree with the layout of Battalion Standing Orders and considered that they should be rewritten. This meant many meetings between the two of us, including one on Christmas morning which did not please my wife!

During this period there was a lot to be done, both work and pleasure. We both loved being able to be in the jungle either to fish, shoot or just to drive the car looking for animals. We were lucky as we again saw tiger, panther, sloth and black bear and many types of deer.

One night we saw an animal, which we could not identify. It was walking along in a deep ditch and looked like a panda with its colour reversed. Pandas, however, do not live in India. The locals said, when I described it to them, that it was called a rintalkin and was both rare and very fierce. A Forest Officer said that he knew of the animal but had never seen one, he confirmed that it was both very fierce and rare. I think that it may have been a honey badger or a near relation.

The world situation was getting worse, but the Japanese were seldom mentioned as a dangerous foe, and the role of the Indian Army fighting outside India was considered to be doubtful, anyhow for some considerable time.

We carried on as we always had done, playing polo and I tried to train the football team for the Gurkha Brigade Cup. As I had started a correspondence course in order to work for the Staff College, I had to keep up with the papers and tests they sent me. This meant working in the evenings, so many invitations had to be refused, but we kept Sundays free for a trip to the jungle.

The C.O. decided that the Battalion should spend the main collective training period in a jungle camp during late November/December. I do not know why this decision was made but I did know that the C.O. was convinced that one day we might find ourselves fighting bandits in strange parts of the world. It was a start but, as no-one had had any experience of living in a jungle under war conditions, we did not learn very much. We were to learn the hard way and to fight a ruthless enemy, the weather and disease, which we did.

The months passed and we continued our work carrying out some Battalion training and the normal basic training such as range work, etc. We spent part of my annual leave in Chakrata, staying at the Chakrata Hotel where I was able to work for the Staff College examination.

On our return to Dehra Dun I was given a vacancy on what was known as 'The Backward Boys' Course' which was run by A.H.Q. Simla for those who hoped to take the Staff College examination. We stayed at one of the Simla hotels and met many old friends, also an uncle of mine. I kept up with my correspondence course and much enjoyed the A.H.Q. course. Joan was able to see several old friends and put up with my working hours.

Towards the end of the course news came through from Waziristan that an Officer had been killed by tribesmen on his way back from Razmak to Wana. It so happened that this Officer was married to my first cousin, but I had never met him.

On our return to Dehra Dun we carried out several Battalion Exercises as we realised that war between Great Britain and Germany was inevitable.

We set forth on a twenty-four-hour exercise in the hills towards Mussourrie and were ordered to leave an N.C.O. in the Lines who would know where we were, in case Brigade Headquarters had orders for us. Sure enough, the N.C.O. found us and handed in a message which ordered the Battalion to return to Dehra Dun and our Battalion Lines at once. We had to wait for about twelve hours when we heard we were at war.

The reader may ask why the wireless was not used to recall us. This was 1939 and we had no wireless sets!

One of the first things we had to do was to mount guards on certain key installations such as electricity supply depots and bridges. The Bridge Guards were mostly found by our 1st Battalion.

Within a very short time after the Declaration of War we received orders to move to Damdil camp on the road from Bannu to Razmak. Joan decided that she would go and stay with her father, who had been recalled to India and was now Chief of Staff of H.E. The Nizam's State Forces at Hyderabad, Deccan.

A well-known Muller was encouraging the Frontier tribesmen to fight and get rid of the British. He clearly considered that the fact the British were at war with Germany provided a golden opportunity for his dreams.

The gentleman concerned had been troublesome for a long time and had earned the nickname of the 'Mad Muller'.

We entrained for Dera Ismail Khan where we transferred from the broad gauge line to the narrow gauge, crossed the Indus bridge and moved very slowly to Banu aboard the 'Heat Stroke' Express, which must hold the record for the slowest train. A friend of mine, in another Gurkha Regiment, was a passenger on this train, when a Tonga (horse and trap) passed the train. My friend leant out of the carriage window and shouted to the engine driver, 'What a disgrace, even tongas can pass.' Whereupon the Driver stopped the train and said that he would not proceed any further until the Sahib withdrew his abuse and apologised!

We reached Bannu, a fortified family station, during the late afternoon and moved to the rest camp where we spent two nights.

The C.O. and Second-in-Command were ordered to report to Damdil Camp and I was ordered to march the Battalion to the first rest camp, where the Second-in-Command would rejoin the Battalion.

That evening, after 'stand-to', the Second-in-Command and I were having a drink with one or two other Officers and G.O.s outside the Mess when the camp was sniped from across a Nullah. The flash of the sniper's rifle had been spotted by one of the sentries and we learnt from one of the camp followers that sniping after dark was a local pastime. However, this time the sniper was lucky as one of his bullets had hit and killed a Battalion Sweeper.

We had been ordered to spend two nights at this camp, so plans were made to give our sniper friend a surprise.

The Sentry, who had seen the rifle flash, indicated where the sniper had been and a medium machine gun was laid-on the position. A G.O.R. with a kukri left our camp after dark to take up a position on a track leading to the sniper's estimated position. All went well to start with and 'our friend' arrived after dark and took up his position, his movements were known to our G.O.R. Unfortunately our ambush then went wrong as the ambusher dislodged a stone which alerted the sniper, who ran away and caused us no more trouble.

The next day the road was open and the C.O. motored back and took over command and we marched on to Damdil and had a meal which had been prepared for us by the 4th G.R.

Damdil was a typical frontier camp, enclosed by barbed wire and a stone wall built of local stone. All tents were also protected by stone walls as a precaution against snipers and attack, but not sandflies. The sandfly appears to suffer from permanent hunger and its bite produced a fever which makes one feel very rotten for a day or two.

Our task was to 'open' the road for convoys to and from Bannu — Razmak at least twice in the week, usually three times a week. We left camp before it was daylight and established ourselves on various commanding hills and withdrew normally just before dark. Whether we had a boring or an exciting day depended on the tribesmen.

We managed to cooperate with our Mountain Gunners and tried to direct their fire on to a tribal tower which was hidden in a deep ravine. I cannot remember if it was ever hit.

After about two weeks we were ordered to carry out a sweep of the area and join up with the Razmak Brigade, who were carrying out a similar task.

We marched to a Bivouac Camp where we met the Commander of

41

Waziristan District who was staying with our Brigadier at a nearby Permanent Levy and Scout Fort. We spent one night in this camp. The next morning we were joined by a squadron of armoured cars and as far as I can remember a troop of light tanks. We already had a troop of mountain artillery. We left the main road and moved along a side road towards our next camp, which we reached during the afternoon. All went well until a water-collecting party moved off to draw water at the water point. They came under heavy rifle fire, but no-one was hit. Our machine guns soon spotted the enemy's position and were ordered to open fire. We had no further trouble that night.

The next day we continued our 'sweep' and came under some quite heavy rifle fire, but once again no-one was hit. We spent the next night holding some strategic hills which dominated the track to our meeting place with the Razmak Brigade.

By now we had been issued with two wireless sets, very flimsy affairs, but portable. During the night one of Signallers sat on one of the sets and it had to be repaired, which was soon done and it was sent to a Company Headquarters. There were other wireless sets on the same frequency and someone asked to speak to the C.O.; the Signaller replied, using all the correct procedure, that he could not be contacted as he was in the lavatory. This bit of information must have been widely known.

We had a little more sniping and then joined the Razmak Brigade in camp for the night. Sniping and, at times, heavier rifle fire continued during the early evening and after dark. I remember only one casualty, a Havildar Mountain Gunner was hit and died later in hospital.

The next day we continued our 'sweep' and returned to Razmak with the Razmak Brigade. At Razmak we were quartered with 8 G.R. who were splendid hosts to Officers and men. We spent a number of days in Razmak and returned to Damdil by road transport.

Meanwhile my left knee was giving trouble and starting to swell. I remember running up a hill to give the C.O. a message and falling on some rocks. When we got back to Damdil I had the knee examined by an M.O. and as result the knee and leg were put in plaster.

After about a week the knee was no better so I was evacuated to hospital in Razmak where I remained for about ten days. After I was discharged from hospital I stayed with 8 G.R. for a few days before returning to Damdil. At Damdil it was found that the knee was still swollen and had only improved a little. I was ordered to take sick leave and to report to the Military Hospital at Secunderabad, which was only a few miles from Hyderabad where I intended to spend my sick leave. After further treatment and massage the knee improved but I was not discharged from treatment. However, I was able to help the State Forces by setting and running some Mountain Warfare Exercises without troops.

During this period we received much kindness from Senior Hyderabad citizens, including both the Princes who were married to very beautiful and charming Persian Princesses. We also received an invitation to a conducted tour of Golcunda Fort and the Curator took us round and gave us an excellent breakfast.

Golcunda Fort had a most interesting history and was the place where the famous Koh-in-Nor diamond was cut.

In due course I received orders to report to the Depot at Dehra Dun and wait for the arrival of the 1st Nepalese Brigade due in a few weeks at Ghangora Camp and to take up the duties of a Junior Supervising Officer with the Mohindra Dal Battalion.

A Medical Board at Dehra Dun declared that my knee was once again sound, but I developed appendicitis and an operation was declared as being very necessary. I had been experiencing considerable pain for some time and after the operation I was informed that the appendix was very nearly closed.

After a couple of weeks I was soon fit again and ready to start with the Nepalese Battalion. The Senior Supervising Officer arrived, he was also 2/2 G.R. and a good soldier, who ended the war as a Major-General. Eventually the Brigade arrived led by a Nepalese Major-General, who was a member of the Nepalese Aristocracy, and a most pleasant man. So were the members of his staff. The British side was under command of a Brigadier, who had commanded a Gurkha Battalion. The Brigadier soon realised that he required a Staff Officer and I was appointed as Staff Captain.

I soon found out the Brigadier was a man who would back his staff and was also a trainer of young Officers.

During an early medical inspection of the Brigade, it was found that a considerable number of men were suffering from a disease called filariasis and it was feared that it might be transmitted to Regular Troops. The outcome was that the Brigade was ordered to move to Dargai Fort in the Malakand. Joan and the S.S.O.'s wife moved to Murree, a hill station on one of the roads to Kashmir, and stayed in an hotel. Murree was within reasonable distance by road from Dargai and we were able to see our wives at weekends. Malakand was then held by a Battalion of 8 G.R. The 2nd Nepalese Brigade were in a camp not far from Abbotabad. The 8 G.R. allowed us to share a large bungalow with a very nice Major and his wife, in Malakand Fort. So Joan moved to a new quarter and spent many hours fishing!

Chapter 7

Two Frontiers

It was amazing how quickly the Nepalese Brigade adopted our Army's standard of hygiene and customs. Their discipline improved every day and Officer standards rose daily. It was not many weeks before the Brigade broke up and selected Battalions were posted to Regular Army Brigades. A new Nepalese Brigade under command of our Nepalese General was to form at Hassan Abdal on a large open plain at the junction of the road from Abbotabad and the trunk road, Rawalpindi and Peshawar.

Units of the new Brigade, still called 1st Nepalese Brigade, were to be one Battalion of the old 1st Brigade and two Battalions of the 2nd Brigade.

We motored off to Hassan Abdal, where we found that the rest house was full, so we collected a tent from those dumped for the Brigade and it was pitched for us by men of the Advanced Party.

There we were with only a view for miles. Army wives conquered most things and we, in a day or so, had a comfortable tented home with a brick cookhouse and the servants we wanted supervised by my faithful Bearer, a man from Garhwal, Sher Singh. Two other families soon joined us.

Our Regular Brigadier was given a new Brigade who were in camp about ten miles from Abbotabad so we were able to visit him and his family a few months later.

I began to feel it was time to return to 2/2 G.R. who were again in Waziristan, so I wrote to their new C.O. I received a letter from him to say that he had already requested my return, but had been told that I was about to be posted elsewhere. I did not see 2/2 G.R. again, except for a short period when they landed at Calcutta after their return from Malaya and P.O.W. Camp in 1945.

Many changes were now taking place. The army in India was expanding and in the Middle East our fortunes were fluctuating. Our 1st Battalion was sent to the Middle East and 2/2 G.R. to Malaya.

The new 1st Nepalese Brigade was broken up and its units sent to join Regular Army Brigades.

I was instructed to move to Abbotabad and supervise the range work for a Nepalese Battalion and then to proceed to Quetta as a student at the Staff College on the fourth War Course.

We left Abbotabad knowing that our family would increase in about six months' time in October 1941; because of this we decided to spend a little more and to travel across some of the hottest parts of India in one of the new air-conditioned railway coaches, which we had to leave at Sibi, the junction for Quetta. We felt the difference in temperature and in the amount of dust.

During the journey from Sibi to Quetta some strange creature stung me on my left forearm. I did not think about it until I had been in Quetta for a couple of days, where we were staying with old Regimental friends. He had a staff appointment in Quetta. I noticed that my arm was swelling up and had become very painful. After six operations and an arm in a sling for a number of weeks, it was decided that the comparatively new drug to India, sulphonamide should be tried as a last attempt to heal the poison. It worked, as it was to do on my chin about a year later in Burma. The Senior Surgeon told Joan that they were considering the removal of my arm if the sulphonamide did not kill the poison.

I much enjoyed the Staff College, in spite of the pain in my arm. Early in October the second major Quetta earthquake took place and caused considerable damage to communications and to the drink ration in the shops, which had just arrived and had been thrown off the shelves. We had a new earthquake-proof bungalow and had nothing broken. Shocks went on for about a week after the main earthquake but in spite of all this our child was nearly two weeks late and did not arrive until 14th October! Our first child, a son.

While at Quetta the Japanese were advancing on all fronts and Pearl Harbour took place. We were having a very bad time both on land and at sea. Hong Kong fell, followed by Malaya and then Singapore. Anyone who lived through those days will know just how dark they were and how very difficult it was to explain to many Indians how we British could be defeated everywhere, when we were such Empire builders and let it be known what a mighty nation we were. Trouble might break out in India, especially if Russia joined the Axis Powers. It was interesting to note that the India Communist Party caused very little trouble once they knew that Russia had sided with the Allies, and it was the same after V.E. Day when Russia declared war on Japan. The question was, where would Japan attack next? Jungles and mountains did not matter to their war machine, so perhaps it could be Burma and then India. So thought public opinion.

As part of our Staff Course we visited various defence works designed to close the passes on the road to India.

One of our exercises was to design a Battalion Defence Position on the route through Baluchistan to Persia. I was looking at my map when an old Baluch came up to me, saluted and said that he had been in a Baluch Regiment so knew I was engaged in laying-out some sort of military position. He added, 'I cannot think why you bother as any enemy are at least three weeks away!'

Quetta and the passes through the mountains to Quetta can be very cold in winter with a wind that can cut through anything. We soon learnt the value of wearing corduroy khaki trousers and needed them.

At the end of my Staff College Course and a day or so after Christmas, we left for the Depot at Dehra Dun where I was told to await further orders.

After twenty-four hours at the Dehra Dun Hotel orders were received to report immediately to Jhansi and to assume the duties of Brigade Major, 63 Indian Infantry Brigade.

We left the next day, which was New Year Day 1942, and arrived at Jhansi during the afternoon of 2nd January, 1942.

We were met at the railway station by the Brigade Staff Captain, an Emergency Commissioned Officer, with little knowledge of being a Staff Captain, but keen to learn. His main consideration was to maintain strict secrecy and to trust no-one. He was quite correct, of course, but it was at times a bit overdone and somewhat difficult to deal with, when he was not prepared to trust the Brigade Clerks because they were Anglo-Indian or for some such reason.

He told us that we had been allocated a bungalow near to the Brigade Office and that he would take us there.

Being India, all our baggage was with us and we soon arrived at our new home. A furniture dealer had furnished the bungalow and said that he would be only too happy to supply anything we wanted or to exchange anything we did not like.

These men had served the Army for so long that they had acquired a knowledge of what Memsahib would want. The necessary servants were engaged and they rapidly learnt that Sher Singh was their 'Boss' and that the Sahib and Memsahib knew India and its customs.

When everything had been done for the present, the Staff Captain suggested that he and I should go to the Club for tea, as he had quite a lot to tell me. We had learnt the Brigadier's name and little else. At the Club my new friend instructed a Club servant to place a table in the middle of the lawn and then to get us tea.

I was given my Brigade Major's armband and told that the Brigade Commander would arrive within the next two days and go off to the Senior Officers' School for a special course. The Units of our new Brigade were all Regular Battalions and were the 1/11th Sikh Regiment, 2/13th Frontier Force Rifles and the 1/10th Gurkha Rifles and were due before the end of the month and other Brigade Troops such as Brigade Signal Section, Field Company, Field Ambulance, Ordnance and Electrical and Mechanical Engineers would be phased in as soon as they were ready. Our task was to train very hard and be ready to move to the Middle East in about seven months' time. I said goodnight to my friend and arranged for him to pick me up the next morning and take me to the Headquarters and Offices of 63 Brigade.

When I got back to our bungalow I found that Joan and Sher Singh had everything under control. I then had a bath and got ready for dinner after a 'Chota Peg' which somehow was ready waiting.

Chapter 8

Jhansi to Burma

The next morning I spent looking round the office seeing that telephones, etc., worked. I also had a visit from a G.S.O.2 at Divisional Headquarters, who said that I could expect our Brigade Commander that afternoon and that he would leave for his course the next day. I was also given some information about 63 Brigade and learnt that our Brigade Troops were all new Units, but there would be time to train them. Other members of the Brigade Staff would arrive in the next few days and a typewriter and paper arrived and I am sure gum arabic, as no office was an office in India without gum arabic!

A Staff car was allocated to Brigade Headquarters closely followed by the Head Clerk and I was told to submit our Indents to Division for necessary stores and equipment as soon as possible.

Things were looking up and I looked forward to the period of training we all required. Establishment tables soon arrived and we then knew what transport we should have — it was mixed M.T. and mule.

The Brigadier arrived at our bungalow during the late afternoon and we both liked him very much. He told us that he had had a look at 'Flag Staff' House but, as he was a bachelor, the annexe was all that he required; he therefore suggested, that he should hand the bungalow over to us and become our 'paying guest'. We agreed and at his request moved house the next day. A move of this nature was not nearly so bad as it sounds. We were very used to rapid moves and had plenty of servants to carry out all the necessary work involved. By the next evening everything was normal again and it would have appeared to a stranger that we had been in the bungalow for several weeks. The

Brigadier went off on his course and we saw him again in about a week's time.

Our Infantry Units arrived between the 5th and 20th January, but no modern weapons and very few stores and equipment. Although we knew the nomenclature of our Brigade Troops and their state of training, we did not know when to expect them. In fact we saw them on 23rd February for the first time.

It was now time to get to know the Commanding Officers of Infantry Units so I visited them as often as I could. They were all very nice and I knew the Commander of 1/11th Sikhs, having met him at Pachmarhi. He kindly introduced me to his Sikh Officers who were very smart men and it was quite clear to me that a British Officer who had known Sikhs all his Service and understood them, and the kind of discipline they understood, was most necessary. The Sikh is a very good soldier and a nice man, but he requires to be worked hard and he likes discipline.

The Brigadier arrived back from his course and the Union Jack was hoisted on the flag staff to show that he was in residence. We soon got to know what the Brigadier liked to eat and life was good for us all.

By this time we had a few more key personnel at Brigade Headquarters such as Clerks and, as luck would have it, our Brigade Ordnance Warrant Officer (B.O.W.O) and some extra staff cars were allocated.

On the 26th January a G.S.O.2 at Division rang me up and said that he was just about to leave his Headquarters as he had an important signal for the Brigade Commander.

He arrived and handed me a signal from A.H.Q which read '63 Bde. will mobilise immediately and prepare to embark for Burma'.

The Brigade Commander was talking to one of the Battalion Commanders in his office so I went in and handed him the message. The remaining C.O.s were sent for and given the new orders. A Brigade Staff Conference was called for that afternoon at which priorities were handed out and Units detailed to produce men for the Defence Platoon and Officers for the appointments of Brigade Orderly Officer, Liaison Officers and Brigade Transport Officer, also Brigade Intelligence Officer and men for the Intelligence Section. There was, of course, no chance of training these Officers and men, so we just had to hope for the best.

Indents for both peace and mobilisation stores, equipment and weapons were made out and very real help given to us by both Division and Area Headquarters. We were a new Formation and therefore had nothing apart from our own personal weapons. We were in need of office equipment such as typewriters, duplicating machine and the necessary stationery. Being an absolutely new formation, Brigade Headquarters had no mess and nothing in the way of knives, forks, spoons, etc. The Brigadier asked Joan if she would produce all that was necessary as none of us could afford the time to shop. She readily agreed and soon had all the items necessary collected and paid for.

We worked hard and wrote out Indents as fast as we could. None worked harder than our B.O.W.O. and Clerks. We soon saw the result of our labours as everything arrived together. Battalions received their modern weapons which included mortars, Sten guns and Bren guns. There was not time for every man to fire a weapon course, but the Brigade Commander was given the use of the Field Firing Area and undertook to give as many men as possible the chance to fire their new weapons.

By now we had received our embarkation orders and knew our ports of embarkation which were Madras for personnel and Calcutta for transport.

Transport Platoons were sent off to the various depots with instructions to collect mules, trucks, etc., and then move to Calcutta under orders of Movement Control.

It says a lot for the discipline and loyalty of the old Indian Army to be able to record that, to my knowledge, there was only one desertion. A man deserted from one of the transport platoons on the way to Calcutta.

We also heard that our Brigade Troops would join the Brigade at Madras.

My wife and son left Jhansi for Hyderabad on 18th February, 1942, and by 0900 hours on 20th February, 1942, the Brigade had left Jhansi.

We became a Brigade Group, that is we were joined by all the other Units required to make a Group by 23rd February, 1942.

Just before our first troop trains reached Madras there had been a practice air raid alarm and the dock labour force, thinking it was the real thing, returned to their homes. The docks, therefore, were without labour and came to a standstill. This gave us a chance to 'shop' for Brigade Headquarters and, through the help of the Area Commander, we purchased a duplicating machine and one or two other items. We, however, were still short of typewriters so I told the Head Clerk to continue to use my own private machine. After the war was over we were instructed to put in claims for items lost due to the war. I claimed for my portable typewriter which I last saw in Jhansi, to be told by some Babu that typewriters were part of Mobilisation equipments and therefore my claim was rejected!

Our date of sailing depended on the return to work of the dock labour. We did not sail until 1600 hours on 27th February, 1942.

While we waited the people of Madras were most hospitable and all Officers were made Honorary Members of their Clubs, where we could enjoy a shower and good food.

I was especially fortunate as the Port Officer, a Captain in the Royal Indian Navy, had served under my father. He and his wife did all they could to make me feel at home.

Brigade Headquarters plus their attached Troops were allocated to the Convoy Commander's ship *Erinpura* where on arrival we found the 1/11 Sikhs, who produced the Zig Zag Sentries (the men who told the ship's Officer of the Watch when it was time to alter the course, as an anti-submarine precaution).

Just before we sailed, a hospital ship arrived from Rangoon and shortly after it had docked a rowing boat left the ship's side and headed for the *Erinpura*.

An R.A.M.C. Officer reported to me, told me that he was a surgeon at one of the well-known London hospitals and had joined up for the war. He added that he had joined as he wished to help the wounded as near the front line as possible, not then be told that his services were not required so he had better return to India with the next batch of wounded. I sent him off to the Commander of our Field Ambulance who took him back to Rangoon. I met him once or twice during the next year or so and he was doing a first-class job.

Out at sea I saw a cruiser and a frigate and asked who they were and was told that the cruiser was H.M.S. *Dorsetshire* and that the frigate, whose name I forget, was a Royal Indian Navy Ship and that they were our escort. They carried out their duties with the help of the cruiser's Walrus aircraft, which carried out sweeps around the convoy. Our transport was about to sail from Calcutta. We were on our way. Our first experience was the black-out and very strict orders about smoking and lights on deck after dark. It was particularly important that no rubbish was thrown overboard.

Nothing of any importance took place that night and we got used to the heat on a blacked-out ship in the Bay of Bengal.

The next morning the Commander of the Convoy sent word that he would like to see me on the Bridge. I went up and was asked if I was any relation to Captain Forteath who the Commander used to know. I said that I was his son. I was then shown the charts we were sailing by and saw that they were signed by my Father. After meeting a number of Ship's Officers, I told them that the last time I had seen the *Dorsetshire* was when she was being built. My Father took a keen interest in a Junior Conservative Party Organisation called, I think, the Junior Imperial and Constitutional League, and he arranged a number of interesting visits for our local branch. One such visit was to Portsmouth dockyard and as I was a member I went too.

I spent a little time watching the Zig Zag Sentries carrying out their duties, then left the Bridge to see what everyone else was doing. Our Brigade Troops were all hard at work at their respective jobs and the Battalion of Sikhs said that all was well. I should add that the weather was good and the sea calm or things might have been different.

That night I was asleep in my cabin when an orderly arrived to say that I was required to report to the Bridge immediately. I went up and was told that the convoy had 'turned about' and was now heading back to India. The cause of this trouble was suspected enemy submarines. I was told to keep this information to myself as it was unconfirmed. As there was nothing I could do, I went back to my cabin and slept till day-break.

During the early hours of 1st March, 1942, we were ordered to 'about turn' and when I came on deck we were once again heading for Rangoon.

We were worried about our transport as it was possible that enemy submarines could be covering the mouth of the river Hoogli. However, they were not attacked and arrived at Rangoon a few hours after we did.

As there was very little that we soldiers could do about submarines, beyond seeing that orders were obeyed, we left the problem in the very capable hands of our sailors.

The day of 3rd March dawned as tranquil as ever and the weather was glorious. As we approached the coast of Burma we saw smoke above the Rangoon river and were told that it came from fires started by a recent enemy air raid on the docks. We soon saw a wonderful sight. The Shwe-Da-Gon Pagoda in Rangoon was caught by the rays of the sun and shone in its golden glory. Such sights as this were not uncommon in Burma and whenever one saw them one realised what a beautiful country it was. It was also a lazy country, which left most of the work to the womenfolk and banditry to the men, who joined various Thakin Bands if it suited them. Europeans, on the whole, liked the country as it offered them a lot. But care had to be taken not to allow soldiers and others to be caught by the 'sloth belt attitude' which was adopted by too many. Whoever considered that an enemy such as the Japanese would dominate both sea and land and sweep into Burma in the way they did? Some did, but a 'prophet is without' etc., ctc.

Just before we sailed up the Rangoon river, two R.A.F. Hurricanes flew over our convoy and escorted us to the docks.

Other curious aircraft were flying around and we were told that they were Chinese flown by American pilots.

We docked at about 1500 hours and were told that disembarkation would start at 1530 hours. Our orders were to unload as many ambulances as we could and by our own efforts as, due to the enemy air raid, all the dock labour had run away. Coupled with ambulances was ammunition. That was the last I saw of my kit.

We were given our Concentration Area, which was Hlaga, to which place we would move by train that night.

The first Battalion to entrain were the 2/13th F.F.R. who were given about two hours to disembark, unload what they could and entrain for Hlaga at Rangoon Central Station. They did it!

Brigade Headquarters and its attached troops were ordered to entrain at 0115 hours on the 4th March, 1942, so we had time to march to the B.A. Football Stadium and to prepare a meal. I sent the Intelligence Section on its first job, to find the railway station and to time how long it took to get there from our present location.

We detrained at Hlaga at about 0200 hours and reached our Concentration Area at 0230 hours and had a sleep near to a rest house, which was to be Brigade Headquarters.

The Brigadier had joined us at the railway station so the Brigade was all present, except for the transport which we were told would move by road and join us at Hlaga as soon as possible. We awoke early on the 4th March, wondering where we were and what was happening. We soon learnt of the River Sittang disaster and how a C.O. and his Adjutant had been murdered while resting on the riverbank after swimming the river: the work of Thakins.

A Brigade Reconnaissance was ordered for the afternoon and the morning spent sorting out our kit and stores. We at Brigade Headquarters tested our Mess!

The Brigadier was ordered to report to the Commander of 17th Indian Division at once at its location south-west of Pegu on the Rangoon–Pegu road. The C.O. 1/11th Sikh was ordered to take charge of the reconnaissance party. We next saw the Brigadier on the 4th March, when he sent for reconnaissance parties.

Up a slight hill from the bungalow we found a large lake which supplied the water for Rangoon. While we were looking at the lake an aircraft flew round us, I think it was a Lysander, and dropped a message which said '200 tanks carrying-out an encirclement at _____'. This was cheerful news as our anti-tank guns had not arrived and there were very few areas which afforded natural cover from tanks.

While we were pondering this problem we spotted the aircraft again and the pilot dropped another message which read 'Reference last message, for tanks substitute elephants'.

We smiled again!

We were just about to carry on with our reconnaissance when a 'runner' arrived from Brigade Headquarters with a message ordering reconnaissance groups to report immediately to the Brigade Commander at 4th Armoured Brigade Headquarters after having contacted the Divisional Commander on the way.

Chapter 9

First Taste of Battle

We met our Brigade Commander at Armoured Brigade Headquarters. This Armoured Brigade had recently arrived from the Middle East and had seen much action. Their way of life gave the impression of battle efficiency, which Units soon adopted after their initial taste of battle. The Units of this Brigade were 7th Royal Irish Hussars and 2nd Royal Tank Regiment.

The Brigade Commander briefed us on the situation, which was bad. The disaster of the River Sittang had just taken place. Our forces had lost a lot of men and equipment on the bank of the river, after the bridge had been blown. It is not for me to give an opinion as to why orders were given to 'blow' the bridge when the majority of our troops were on the enemy side of the river, it is sufficient to say that it was 'blown' and many men could not swim, nor had they any idea or what to use to help them across a large river. This was one of our first priorities when we were given the opportunity a few months later.

Each Unit Reconnaissance Party was looked after by a Unit of 48 Indian Infantry Brigade, at whose location it spent the night. Our Brigade Headquarters went to 48 Brigade Headquarters where we were billeted in the Law Courts and opposite the Field Ambulance, not far from a fire started by incendiary bombs dropped during a Japanese air raid.

The ground was very hard and when incendiary bombs burst, pieces of phosphorus bounced like ping pong balls, setting fire to tinder-dry grass, wood, etc. We had one or two bad attacks when pieces of phosphorus landed on wounded men lying on stretchers and set fire to their clothing.

After the Sittang battle morale was not as high as it could be and who would expect it to be anything else. Before we had a meal at 48 Brigade Headquarters Mess, the Brigadier took us up to the 1/4th G.R. Command Post where the Commanding Officer (later a Chindit General) briefed us on the enemy, their weapons and ability to use the jungle especially for what was to become their well-known encirclement movement. I saw no signs of movement in the direction of the enemy. However, I learnt a lot about fighting Japanese and their allies the Thakins and members of Chandra Bose's gang. I spoke to one or two G.O.R.s and asked them what they thought of the enemy.

I almost always got the same reply: 'He has some very good weapons and his infantry gun does a lot of damage. He must also be a very strong man as he can throw a grenade a very long way.'

This last remark puzzled me until I learnt that the Jap had a weapon called a grenade launcher which threw a grenade further than a man could, but with less accuracy. The infantry gun was a good weapon and was fired over open sights. Luckily the explosive used in Japanese shells was not very effective. Their weapons made a lot of noise but were not nearly so effective as ours. I can vouch for my last statement as later I was to be bombarded by 3″ mortars, ours, which the enemy had captured.

I also heard a lot of adverse comment about the Civil Administration in Burma, in particular about two hills which had religious connections and it was made clear that we should avoid these hills in order not to upset the Burman. When dawn broke the enemy had manhandled two guns up the hills and then had proceeded to fire at our men, over open sights.

I was not there at the time so cannot confirm or deny the story. I tell the story to show the state of morale and that we had not learnt that it must be total war when battle starts, it and it alone must dominate our thoughts and actions.

After we had had a meal the Brigadier told me to try and find some transport to take me back to the Advanced Elements of 63 Bde. Pegu had a number of large fires burning, but the main road appeared to be without any major problems. I stopped a number of vehicles and asked them for a lift back down the road, but none were going as far as Divisional Headquarters and most of the drivers were looking for somewhere to park for the night which was free from fire. My orders were to take over Command of the Brigade until the 1/11 Sikhs arrived, then I was to hand over to their Second-in-Command. After trying to find a vehicle for about an hour, I decided to report my failure to the Brigadier.

While I was waiting at the side of the road, I had my first real meeting with the C.O. of the 2/5 R.G.R., who I had first met in the Malakand several years before. I did not, of course, know at our meeting in Pegu that the man I now met would become a family friend, Godfather to one of our sons and would have a profound influence on my life. I met a first-class soldier.

A jeep drew up beside me and I saw that it was driven by a Lieut-Colonel of the 2/5th R.G.R.

He asked me where a certain Gurkha Officer was. I told him that I did not know this Officer and that although I was an Officer in a Gurkha Regiment I was B.M. of 63 Ind. Inf. Bde. He said very little in reply and drove off. He was known to have a bad temper and, if it had not been for the war, might even have been forced to retire as a Major as he spoke his mind and said what he thought to whomsoever he was talking. He also liked a drink or two — who does not? He only showed signs of temper with me once and I deserved it. Our comradeship was to grow in the months to come and we had great trust in each other.

I went back and told the Brigadier that nothing in the way of transport was going back as far as 63 Bde. until daylight. I went to bed and spent one of the worst nights I had in Burma! I had no blanket, so lay on the wire springs of the bed in my room. Mosquitos attacked me, aided by sandflies from the direction of the roof and upwards through the springs!

I was up at daylight on 6th March, 1942, as firing had started below my window. I looked out and saw a Gurkha firing at something I could not see. The G.O.R. was lying in a flower bed of what looked like forget-me-nots. I went out to find out what it was all about and was told by the G.O.R. that he was firing at Burmans and that there were also Japs.

63 Bde. had received orders to recce the area in the vicinity of the Railway Station ready for the Bde. to occupy. However, we soon learnt that the Japs had got there first, having carried out one of their encircling movements through the Jungle during the night.

So we awaited further orders. A feature of South Burma was the early morning mist which reduced visibility to a few yards. No-one had told us about this and at first we were a little worried about it, but we soon learnt and used it as cover and expected it to clear about 7.30 a.m.

At breakfast the Brigade Commander decided that he would remain at Pegu while the rest of us got back to the Brigade.

At 0800 hours, 6th March, 1942, a Japanese recce aircraft came over and was shot down. At about the same time three of the 7th Armd.Bde. tanks arrived with orders to take us back to 63 Brigade. At the last moment the Brigadier decided to join us and orders were received that we should transfer to carriers and any of us who could not find a place in a carrier were to remain at 48 Bde. H.Q.

We left Pegu at about 1100 hours in two 1/4 G.R. carriers escorted by two tanks which led.

Our carrier was driven by the Carrier Officer 1/4th G.R. and carried the Brigadier, O.C. 1/10 G.R., myself and three G.O.R.s 1/4th G.R., one of whom had to sit manning a Bren gun on the outside of the carrier as there was no room inside.

The second carrier was driven by a G.O.R. 1/4th G.R. and carried O.C. 1/11 Sikhs, O.C. 2/13 F.F.R., the Adjutant 2/13 F.F.R., R. Tank Sergeant, G.O.R. 1/4th G.R.

About two miles from Pegu we ran into an ambush. A cart had been placed across the road. However, the ditch on either side of the road was not very deep and the tanks, who drew no fire, led the way down into the ditch and continued on their way.

We followed, but as soon as we became an open target fire broke out from a sniper in a tree and also from the right-hand road ditch. Carrier no. 2 stopped on the road. Sniping was by automatic weapon as well as rifle fire from the ditch. We were all wounded except the G.O.R. who was sitting with a Bren gun outside the carrier.

Somehow the driver managed, in spite of a bullet in his cheek, to get the carrier out of the ditch and to turn it towards Pegu. Firing continued. We were able to signal to no. 2 carrier to follow us and return to Pegu. This signal, which I gave on orders of the Brigadier, was seen by those in no. 2 carrier, but they did not follow, why it was not known for certain, but we were of the opinion that a grenade of some sort, or a small mortar bomb, had been fired into the carrier.

It should be remembered that at this stage of the Burma Campaign we knew very little about the Japs or their weapons.

The O.C. 1/10th G.R. was in a bad way as a number of bullets had passed through my arms and lodged in him. I was also wounded in the face. I did not realise at the time how lucky I was to be alive.

We got back to Pegu and reported to 37 Fd. Amb. who were most kind to us.

I now learnt a little about the effect of war upon men. While we were waiting to be seen by an M.O., I took off my bush shirt which was stiff with blood and removed the small photograph case which was in my breast pocket and found signs which indicated that it had stopped shrapnel from entering my chest and possibly other organs. I have used it as my St. Christopher since that date. I let the shirt lie on the floor. A wounded G.O.R. who was sitting close to me started to curse two I.O.R.s. I asked the Gurkha what was wrong and he replied, 'These two', pointing towards the I.O.R.s, 'have just said "The Major (me) is not looking, let's steal his shirt". I am not having that sort of thing!' I thanked him and had a few words with him and then went in front of the M.O., who was Comdg. 37 Fd. Amb. and an Irishman of great ability as an Army doctor and a man I was to get to know very well in the months to come.

While waiting in the waiting room I saw a badly wounded man lying on a bench. I thought that he could be a high caste Gurkha and asked somebody who he was and was told that he was a Japanese soldier who had been captured by the Hussars. I took him a cup of tea and he made signs that he wanted a cigarette, which he got. The information which this man gave on interrogation was most instructive. I saw quite a lot of him during the journey to Mandalay.

I was what was classified as 'walking wounded', with a jaw stuck together with plaster, a knee and both arms bandaged.

After I had been patched up, the Fd. Amb. C.O., the Intelligence Officer 1/10GR and I went over to the 48 Bde. Mess to see if we could have a cup of tea or something stronger. The I.O. and I had been to school together and he had been left at Pegu when we set off in the morning.

As we finished our tea a Jap air raid took place on the Fd. Amb. and A.A. Gun position which was not far away.

The O.C. Field Ambulance and my friend decided to see what damage had been done so they went to the bungalow door in time to receive the contents of a Jap air bomb. The C.O. was badly wounded in the stomach (his life was saved, he told me later, by his old appendicitis scar) and my old friend was killed. I took his gold signet ring off his finger and put his silver cigarette case in my pocket. Many months later I met a man who was leaving the Burma Front and going on to a part of Assam, where he said he was bound to meet my friend's brother whom we both knew, so he would undertake to give him the ring and the silver cigarette case. I do not know if they were ever received. I saw my friend buried in the Mess garden and was then sent to Pegu Civil Hospital and looked for somewhere to sleep.

I found a bed on which I put something to show that it was reserved and set off to find the Brigade Comd., who had lost an eye and was resting in the same Ward. I then realised that I had had nothing to eat since tea, which consisted of a cup of tea and a biscuit, but thought that I could do nothing about it. Just then the 7th Armd. Bde. Padre came down the Ward; when he got to me he asked if he could do anything for me and I told him that, owing to the bandages, I was quite unable to open my 'flies' and that the situation was getting desperate! I also asked him where I could get something to eat. He dealt with both situations and I had a ration biscuit and a banana. I soon got fed up with lying on my bed, so I decided to walk around for a while and try to find out what the situation was, as there was quite a lot of firing.

Much to my astonishment I came across a troop of 25 Pdr. Guns deployed not far away under the command of a cheerful young man. I asked him who they were and I am fairly certain that he said Essex Yeomanry. What I know he said was, 'You could do with a drink, sit down and I will get you one!'. Then he added, 'We are about to engage a target so get back from the guns.'

The drink arrived — a whisky! I watched the guns engage their target, said goodnight to my kind friends and went back to bed.

Chapter 10

Evacuation

The next morning we were put into ambulances for evacuation down the road towards Rangoon, thence to Hmawbi and I presume Tharrawaddy which was then Railhead.

We left under cover of the early morning mist and had reached about the same place as the previous day's ambush, when we were stopped and told that 48 Bde. was about to clear a wood, on the right of the road, of enemy.

We saw the other carrier in the ditch half over on its side. There were no signs of its occupants.

While we were waiting in the ambulance, which contained the Brigadier, myself and the Officer driver of our carrier the previous day, all walking wounded, also two stretcher cases, the C.O. 1/10 G.R. and the C.O. of the Field Ambulance, we saw a party of Japanese come out of the wood and head for our ambulance. The three of us who could walk won a number of medals for the high jump, long jump and sprinting as we left the ambulance for the road ditch. We next saw a Japanese soldier armed with an automatic weapon move to the open end of the ambulance and fire a burst of fire at the two stretcher cases. We then decided to move up the road and found ourselves in the area of what should have been 48 Bde. Command Post, but we found the O.C. 2/5 R.G.R. was conducting the battle and I saw that he was wounded in both legs. I asked him if I could do anything to help and he replied, 'Open an ammunition point', which I did.

I then saw the 1/4 G.R. preparing to attack the wood on the far side of the road and realised that they intended to use their kukris. They charged across

63

the road and entered the wood. A short while later they came back and it was evident that they had used their kukris, as they were cleaning them on the grass bank. It was the only kukri charge I saw during the Campaign and the men had a curious blood lust in their eyes. The charge cleared the wood and it was soon apparent that the enemy had withdrawn, although some fighting continued for a short time.

My Brigadier, who was lying at the side of the road, said, 'It is time for us to get to somewhere where we can get our wounds looked at.'

We found a Bren Gun Carrier and, with other wounded, climbed in. We had not travelled very far when we were stopped and told that the road was ambushed. So we got out of our extremely hot transport and I asked a British soldier where the ambush was. He indicated the area and added that there was a Japanese sniper, up a tree, not far away. I told him to loan me his Tommy gun and went to have a look for myself. I found nothing. By now ambulances were moving down the road so we each got into one of them and reported to 17 Div. Headquarters where the Div. Commander and G.S.O.1 met me and told me to get to a Dressing Station as soon as I could.

I do not remember how the Brigadier got from Div.H.Q. to the 7th Armoured Brigade Main Dressing Station, which was situated at the crossroads at Taukyan, as I do not remember seeing him until later that day. We had one or two badly wounded cases in our ambulance and we were heading for the crossroads when four Hurricane aircraft flew down the road from the direction of the enemy. We did not take any particular notice as we had seen the R.A.F. markings. However, a few minutes later the same aircraft let fly with everything they had got on to the mixed bag of civilians, women, children and men from Rangoon as well as soldiers, wounded or fit. Rangoon had been evacuated and the Japanese had established another road block near Hmawbi and a few miles north of Taukyan. I next saw a very smart Officer take charge of the situation and direct traffic off the road. It was the Commander-in-Chief. He put our ambulance under cover and off the road and we waited for another air attack, which never came. We heard later that the Hurricanes were from Singapore.

Someone told us to report to the 7th Armoured Brigade M.D.S. which we did and found a splendid organisation. An operating theatre was in a tent and was dealing with casualties, there were rows of stretchers ready for the wounded and a long table was laid for dinner!

After I had been examined I was allocated a stretcher for the night and told that Mess would be at x hours, by the Mess Sergeant who added that we would all receive a drink before dinner!

The O.C.M.D.S. outlined the situation to as many Officers as could walk and told us that the Japanese road block at Hmawbi had not been broken, so we would remain where we were.

I saw an ambulance enter our area and park so I went to see who it was, to my surprise it was O.C. 1/10 G.R. and O.C. 37 Fd Amb. whom we had last seen being shot at by the Japanese. This 'marksman' had missed them both at 0' feet range and his bullets had passed between their stretchers and the ambulance seat. Almost impossible to believe, but it is true.

They both refused any food so I left them to rest and said that I would see them again before I went to sleep. In the meantime, the stretcher on my right was occupied by an Officer of the 2/5 R.G.R. who had a piece of mortar bomb in his stomach. Our Brigadier was as comfortable as he could be and, after seeing the two friends in the ambulance, I went to bed. The operating theatre was a few yards away and surgeons worked non-stop. Soon after I lay down I could hear firing and the badly wounded Officer asked what it was and how far away.

Nothing very much happened until about 2.00 a.m. when I was awakened by someone tripping over my stretcher. I thought he was an I.O.R. and told him to watch where he was going. I then saw that there were lots of soldiers walking through the Field Ambulance, many looked into the operating theatre, but the surgeons just carried on. I then pretended I was asleep!

The Japanese was a man who, in those days, had very little initiative and by the time the troops had reached Taukyan they were about six hours late on schedule for the capture of Rangoon. Therefore they had to press on and not bother about anything else.

At daybreak we heard that the road block had not been broken and the fires from the oil refinery at Rangoon were filling the morning sky with thick black smoke. After some breakfast we saw the C-in-C enter the Field Ambulance. He left after a talk with the C.O. All walking wounded Officers were told to report to the Mess, where the C.O. told us that the enemy were still holding their road block and that the Gloucesters and the Cameronians had heavy casualties.

The Cameronians had only recently had the River Sittang Battle and had taken a lot of casualties.

We were then told that it was the intention of the C-in-C to break out of the present situation and, having abandoned the transport, to cut across country and pull back as far as he could. This meant that the wounded would have to be abandoned and that was that.

I went over to a batch of wounded Officers who were stretcher cases and gave them the news. One of the wounded, who was a Lieut-Colonel, said that he would not allow himself to be captured. He then turned to me and said, 'This is an order, I want your promise that you will not allow me to be taken as a prisoner of war and that you personally will shoot me.'

I too had no intention of being captured and had earmarked a vehicle which I intended to 'borrow' and see how far I could get across country. So I told my wounded friend of my plan and got his 'blessing' and once again his orders about shooting him, if necessary. I then went off to consider my plan and to tell my Brigadier about it. He said that he would come too.

Chapter 11

Evacuation Down the Line

The 8th March, the anniversary of our wedding, started with a lot of enemy bombing and machine gun fire from the air. There were no signs of our aircraft either captured by the Japanese or R.A.F. or Chinese. We heard at about 1130 hours that the road block had been lifted and that the enemy had faded away. Orders were given to assemble a convoy of ambulances for the wounded to be evacuated to the Main Dressing Station at Tharrawaddy and we left at about 1230 hours and reached the M.D.S. during the late afternoon.

We were told that an ambulance train would take us to hospital in Prome early the next morning.

In the meantime, ambulances had to be turned and dressings checked. A splendid Lancastrian M.O. was in charge who never stopped working. He told us that the last thing that he had expected was the arrival of our convoy. I told him that my back was sore and in his very broad accent he told me to take off my shirt. He had a look and announced that I had, 'Piece of shrapnel in my back and that it was pussin.' He then proceeded to remove it.

I was sitting on the ground with the Brigadier and our carrier driver at the time of the Ambush, wondering if and how we could find something to eat, when a B.O.R. came up and said that he would act as our Batman. We said that would be splendid, so he went off and came back with a blanket for us to sit on and announced that he would now find some food. He turned up again with some biscuits and bananas.

In the meantime, one of my bandages required attention so I asked a Corporal in the Cameronians if he could put the bandage on my arm again,

67

which he did and, while he was doing so, someone enquired what his name was. He replied that his name was 'so and so', an Irish name. The Officer who had asked the question then said — an Irishman in a Scottish regiment? 'Oh no,' replied the Corporal — 'Belfast!' He had hardly said this when some more wounded came in and our Corporal was told that his brother had been killed at the Hmwabi road block.

Eventually we all got down to the railway station, including our new Batman, and found the ambulance train ready for us. The Sergeant in charge of the train told the Brigadier and myself to get into his compartment and that we would find a bottle of whisky in his greatcoat pocket. The Brigadier poured out a drink for us both and I was so tired I fell asleep at once and do not remember the train leaving at 0500 hours on 9th March, 1942.

We arrived at Prome about mid-morning and the Brigadier and I thanked the O.C. Train for allowing us to use his compartment, and then went in search of some transport to take us to hospital and found a number of ambulances drawn up in the station yard. On the way we met a European who asked us what was wrong with the modern Army, as in his day in the last war they did not retreat. I was just about to say a few words when the Brigadier stepped in and said, 'Leave him, George, he is not worth bothering about.'

The ambulance convoy took us to a large building, which I think was Prome College, where things were well organised and we had a cup of tea. The Brigadier was taken off to a small room and about five of us were taken to another room, where we found a very badly wounded Major of the Cameronians. He had received his wounds at the Sittang and was by now suffering enough to become delirious.

We were told to select a bed and have a rest until the M.O. came to see us. I found that my next-door neighbour was one of two brothers I used to know — he had been shot in the head.

We had not been very long on our beds when the Cameronian Major demanded a runner as he had a message for the C.O. I went over to see what I could do. I was told to write down the message and to deliver it in person. I proceeded to write something, then left saying I was on my way. I had been on my bed for some twenty minutes or so, talking to the man I knew from Fleet, when there was another shout of 'Runner' from the Cameronian Major, so I again went to see him.

This time he said that he wanted the message for the C.O. read back to him. I listened as carefully as I could. The Major spoke very little sense, but I was able to write something down and was able to repeat it which appeared to satisfy the poor man.

Shortly afterward we were told that our ward was ready for us so we walked upstairs to our beds. A little while later we heard that the Cameronian Major had died a peaceful death.

The next day I met the London surgeon who had come aboard our transport at Madras and, after he had examined my wounds, stated that I should soon be fit for active service again and he then asked me if I thought that I was sufficiently recovered to return in a day or so. I said I was but that I should prefer that all wounds had healed before I returned, as I did not want to risk infection. He agreed.

That afternoon we were told to expect an important visitor so we had to remain in bed. Our visitor proved to be the C-in-C. He had a talk with me and he asked if I was married and, if so, where my wife was living. I told him and his reply was, 'I shall be in this hospital for the next thirty minutes, if you can write a letter to your wife and have it ready for me by the time I am ready to go, I shall see that she gets it.'

When he came back the letter was ready, written on three pages of a note book, but there was no envelope or stamp. The A.D.C. was told to find an envelope and told to include the letter with the official mail to be handed over to the R.A.F. aircraft that evening.

This letter made life clearer for Joan, who now knew that I was alive and wounded and that my wounds would soon be healed. Thanks to 'Man Management' and kindness Joan was saved much anxiety as the next 'Casualty List' published in the Indian daily newspapers reported me as killed-in-action, not wounded.

Later that evening a large number of us were told that we would leave the next day for Mandalay and would travel by river steamer up the Irrawaddy river.

We left Prome on the 11th March by river steamer which had a 'flat' (barge) tied along side. On the two 'ships' were a total of 200 sick and wounded, including the wounded Japanese I had met at Pegu. He was sitting on a bollard under the eye of a Gurkha with a drawn kukri. The Brigadier and I, also my friend from Fleet, were given cabins.

Just before we left, two Staff Officers came aboard and I was delighted to meet one of the Directing Staff of my course at the Staff College, Quetta.

The Captain of the river steamer told the Brigadier that because of enemy air activity, he had been given orders that he would tie up mid-stream at night and not use his search lights, which normally would have been used for night navigation. This would mean that the journey to Mandalay would take longer than usual.

We arrived at Mandalay on the 18th March and found that very little had been laid on. We were directed to the hospital which was located in Fort Dufferin.

The journey up the river was uneventful so far as the Japanese were concerned. At Chauk, which was occupied by the Burma Oil Company staff, laboratories, etc., we were met by the senior member of the Company at Chauk, who kindly asked the Brigade Commander and myself to have a bath and then dinner with him and his no. 2 at his bungalow.

Both men were very worried as all families had left by road for India two days before and they had had no word from any of them.

They said that they and the remainder of the staff and work force were waiting for orders to blow up the oil fields and connected equipment and then start walking to India. In the meantime, would we consider that the club and its contents was ours for as many sick and wounded who could leave the steamer and flat. This included the contents of the bar and cellar. The wounded and many sick had a very welcome break and the kindness of our hosts was very much appreciated by all ranks. I have never met any of our hosts again but, should any of them ever read this account, will they please accept my grateful thanks.

During the journey I developed some kind of fever which lasted for about forty-eight hours. I thought that it was malaria but a doctor said it was not and he thought it was some sort of reaction to the last few days.

We got to Mandalay Hospital and found that the Japanese Airforce had been there before us. Theobaw's Palace was a shambles and looked like anything else after bombing, certainly not a thing of beauty. The hospitals cooks, sweepers, etc., had run away. In fact it was chaos.

We learnt that Thakins had tried to get into the Fort a couple of nights before, but that they were unable to force open the gates. The hospital already had some patients and the young Anglo-Burmese nurses were working like Trojans under their Matron, who was a British nurse and a member of the Minto Nursing Service of pre-war Burma and a very splendid woman she was. We soon realised that something was wrong with the nursing staff and found out that they were terrified of another Thakin attack. The hospital was housed in sheds and there was no outside lighting.

The night nurses had to walk from ward to ward in pitch darkness and were terrified of being attacked. There was only one thing to do and that was to organise Officer Night Patrols to accompany the nurses.

I pause awhile to mention these nurses. Most were Anglo-Burmese girls of eighteen or nineteen and I met several as the Campaign went on. The U.S.

Military Forces had many of these girls. They manned Forward Dressing Stations and Operating Theatres and were utterly dedicated to their work. One night I was on patrol with a nurse when I came across one of the girls crying her heart out. I asked her what the matter was, she replied that she had just lost a B.O.R. who had dysentery and had been doing well. I have heard very little about these girls and their loyalty and devotion and would like to say 'Thank you', even after all these years since the war ended.

As well as the Officer Patrols, any other ranks who were fit enough were organised as 'Defenders' of the Fort walls and gate. I am glad to say that there was never any reason to use our improvised force.

The Brigadier and my friend from Fleet were evacuated to India by air and I never saw either of them again. My friend was killed in the Middle East and most of the remaining Officers were posted to Maymyo on the 28th March with orders to report to the Convalescent Home for Officers, which had just opened in Maymyo. We left Mandalay early in the morning and went up the hill by train and must have reached Maymyo at about 11.00 a.m. We asked the way to the Convalescent Home and nobody had ever heard of such a place. However, we found a Gharri driver who said that he thought he knew where it was. We got into two Gharris and arrived at an empty bungalow whose late owners were on their way to India. We selected two rooms which had beds, a double bed in one room and a single in the other. There were other bedrooms, but all the other rooms were empty. I took the room with the single bed, the other three Officers had a double bed and little else.

I then said to my companions that we would go to the Club and see what we could get to eat. Apart from some strawberries and a pineapple I had bought on the journey, the last meal I had had was supper the night before we left Mandalay.

We found the Club and went to see the Secretary to find out if we could become members. We could, but we were told we could have nothing to eat as all food was strictly reserved for Regular Club members. We asked the Secretary where we could get something to eat and he told us the whereabouts of a Chinese Restaurant. We left the Club wishing the Secretary the very worst, as all we required was scrambled eggs. Outside the restaurant was a pit and in this hole was a bamboo contraption to represent an anti-aircraft gun. The Burmese 5th Column would have reported its location and the fact that it was a fake to the Japanese almost as soon as it was put in position. We got a very reasonable meal and went back to the bungalow.

We had not been in the bungalow very long when we heard someone shouting and found a Padre standing in the hall. He told us that the Home was

71

not due to open until the next day and that he and his wife would run the Home. He said that he would get more furniture in the way of beds, chairs and blankets, etc., and if we could manage to feed ourselves that night, he would organise meals from breakfast the next day. He did everything he said he would do and we then met his delightful family, consisting of his wife and three young children.

They moved into the bungalow next door on the next day and made it known that anyone leaving for India could drop clothes, etc., at the Convalescent Home. I managed to get hold of a pair of ladies pink silk knickers (of large size!) which I wore as pyjamas for many nights, in fact until they were thrown away by my wife on my first leave.

The next day several more Officers arrived at the Home, including the Staff Captain of 63 Bde. I gave him a spare bed in my room. Furniture was arriving in large quantities and by that night we had most things.

We went off to the Club to see if we could get a drink on the night of the 25th and then went there on most evenings. I cannot remember where we had a meal, but think that the rule about temporary members not being allowed any food had been cancelled after our visit earlier in the day.

As far as we could see, the only difference between conditions in peace and war was that whisky was rationed and each member was given a number of whisky tickets for the day. Otherwise people acted as if the enemy was miles away instead of in the country and advancing. The Governor and his staff were in Maymyo and the Club was very well attended.

A lot of people, European and Indian, should have been told to move out of Burma as they were in a few weeks' time, to cause a refugee problem and in some cases it was not possible for troops to withdraw quite so rapidly as it would have been advisable for Commanders to order.

Maymyo was a beautiful place with splendid trees and some very pretty gardens. After the daily, routine air raid which we spent in slit trenches, we went our own way until lunch. Thanks to the kind people who were running the Convalescent Home it became more comfortable every day and we were given more furniture, crockery, etc.

More people arrived daily, including a very amusing American who had been a Vice Consul in one of the Embassies in China. I was able to make a contract with an Indian Gharri owner, who I called Albert. He came for me everyday about 10.15 a.m. and took me to the Botanical Gardens, where I tried to identify the many birds, including pheasants. I also enjoyed the flowers, shrubs and trees.

One day I came across a road named Forteath Drive or Ride. My father told me, after the war was over, that it was named after my uncle who was a Forest Officer in Maymyo before being posted to the Central Provinces in India.

Albert wanted two things, the first was a felt hat of the type worn by Gurkha soldiers and men of the Burma Rifles.

The other was that I should tell him when he and his family should leave Burma and join the long steam of Indians returning to India, many of whom never made the journey through sheer exhaustion, starvation and diseases such as cholera. Albert got both his wishes and we said goodbye to each other a few days before I left for 17 Div. Albert was very worried about the Burmans he would meet on the road. Burmans and Indians did not like each other, as the Indian worked hard and thus controlled most of the commerce in Burma. The Burman is a cheerful, idle man as I have said elsewhere.

Indians were attacked with 'Dars' on their long trek and a large number murdered. Later I saw many refugees on the march, in fact we protected them as far as we could by Carrier Patrols with orders to shoot any Burman who was suspected of attacking Indian refugees. The most distressing thing I saw was mothers throwing their children into the road ditch as they could not carry them any further. British women and children also did the long trek, helped by 'Elephant Bills', wonderful elephants, including the magnificent Bandoola. I never heard of any attack on British women and children, but heard details of the march from cousins of my wife, who did the trek with two young children and also from Elephant Bill and his wife.

I had reported to Army Headquarters several times since my arrival in Maymyo to find out my future posting. Eventually I was passed 100 per cent fit and was posted as Brigade Major 48 Indian Infantry Brigade, 17 Ind. Div. The Brigade was being commanded by the O.C. 2/5th R.G.R. who I had last seen on the road south of Pegu. The Brigade was made up of three Gurkha Battalions, 1/4th G.R., 2/5 R.G.R. and 1/7th G.R. All Battalions were very under-strength and they had all suffered heavy casualties at the Sittang and other battles. The Brigade was now holding Taungdwingi where 17th Div. Headquarters were also located.

I was given orders to leave Maymyo on the 16th April and move to Mandalay by train where I should be given transport to 48 Bde. I was also told that I should be accompanied by the new C.O. 1/3rd G.R. and a Captain R.A. who was posted as Temporary Staff Captain to 48 Bde, also two officers of 48 Bde., who had been sick and had been ordered to report to me and move forward under my orders. I saw one of these Officers during the afternoon of 15th April and I told him to report to the railway station with his friend at a specific time on the 16th April, the next day. I never saw either of them again.

Chapter 12

Return to Soldiering

The next day, April 16th, 1942, I went down to the railway station and met the new C.O. of the 1/3 G.R. who I knew and the Temporary Staff Captain of 48 Bde., a 'Gunner'.

I looked for the other two Officers, who were under orders to join our party, but there were no signs of them.

The journey down the hill was without incident until we reached a station about six miles from Mandalay where we were told to leave the train, as owing to an air raid it was not possible to proceed any further. We were also told that there was no transport of any kind to Mandalay.

However, thanks to some people who were looking after refugees, we found a fire engine about to return to Mandalay and the crew told us to climb on board and 'hang on tight'. We saw the results of recent air raids, but arrived at Fort Dufferin without incident and spent the night at the Transit Camp. No-one had any idea as to how we could move forward from Mandalay. Later we were told that the Chinese, who had a supply depot in the Fort, would take us early next morning to Meiktila, where we would find the supply depot for 17th Div.

We reported to the Chinese very early the next day and were told to get into a half-empty truck and started a 'hair-raising' trip to Meiktila at great speed. The roads in Burma, because of the monsoon, have deep ditches on either side. Just before we reached Kyaukse, we turned sharp left, regardless of the ditch, and entered the jungle. I cannot remember how we crossed the ditch or eventually how we got back on to the road, but we did! The driver of our truck managed to explain to us that the convoy had been told to get off the road and to get under cover as enemy aircraft were very active. We saw no signs of any aircraft, either ours or the enemy. The Chinese had been fighting the Japanese for many months and knew a lot about avoiding bombs and machine gun fire from enemy aircraft.

During the afternoon we reached Meiktila and found our supply depot on the shores of the lake. The C.O. of the depot was most kind and we were given a good meal and told that 48 Bde. Supply Section would take us forward the next day, 18th April. That evening I met our Bde. Supply Officer and we became very great friends, in fact he is my daughter's Godfather, and I was best man at his wedding in England after the war.

The next day we left early, using the line of the railway track to Taungdwingi. The Sappers had removed the railway lines so we had a good straight road to 17 Div. When we reached Taungdwingi we reported to H.Q. 17 Div. and we were told where to find our units. We had arrived at last, perhaps after a journey which did not resemble the pre-War Promotion Examination diagrams of how ex-wounded were returned to their units? But we learnt that one of the essentials of war is the ability to improvise and make the best of it.

48 Bde. consisted of 2/5 R.G.R., 1/4 G.R. and 1/7 G.R., all of which were well under-strength and still suffering from their losses at Sittang.

An extra Unit was also under command, the 1/3 G.R., which consisted of about six British Officers, a similar number of G.O.s and a handful of G.O.R.s, about twenty in number.

The Bde. was under command of the man I had last seen on the road to Pegu, shot through both legs. I reported to the Brigadier and was put in the picture and told that Taungdwingi was to become the final stand from which there would be no withdrawal. I was also asked if I knew a Chinaman from a Japanese, as somewhere on our front was a Chinese Infantry Battalion which had become separated from the Chinese 5th Army and had been ordered to join 48 Bde.

We luckily had an Officer in charge of the Bde. Transport, who had been an Officer of the Custom Service in China and could speak the Chinese language, or one of the main dialects, so he had been sent forward to contact the 2/187 Regiment of Chinese and lead them to 48 Bde. They arrived that night.

I had a talk with the acting Bde. Major and Staff Captain, both Officers of the Royal Artillery, who were under orders to return to their Units as soon as possible. They both left the next day.

There was little to be done for the rest of the daylight hours, so I spent the time getting to know the Brigade Staff. To my surprise the Head Clerk was Head Clerk of 63 Bde. The staff happened to be all Scotsmen, except for the R.

Signals Officers, both of whom were English and much liked by us all. The Senior Signals Officer was later to be a Scot and renamed. But that is a separate story!

The next day, April 20th, 1942, I awoke early and had a word with the Brigade Intelligence Officer, who had been a tea planter in Assam before the war and had employed Gurkha labour, so he could speak to the men. He himself was an Officer in the 7th Gurkha Rifles and came from Ayrshire.

He told me that he went out daily with a Carrier Patrol to do what he could to protect the Indian refugees from the Burmese. The Brigade Commander, who came from near Oban and was an Officer in the 5th Royal Gurkha Rifles, was one of the best linguists, so far as Nepalese was concerned, that I ever met. One of his chief worries at that moment was the fact that he had lost his pipe and in any case there was no tobacco, so ground-up cigarettes had to be smoked.

I told the Intelligence Office (I.O.) the sad story and said, 'See what you can do during your patrol.'

It had been arranged that I should meet all the Battalion Commanders and they had decided that we should walk round Taungdwingi and look back at the Defence Position. On one 'Front' stood the jail containing its 'inmates' and Divisional Headquarters had the key. We had been ordered not to let the prisoners out until the Brigade was ordered to withdraw.

As far as we knew Taungdwingi was to become the Tobruk of Burma and there would be no withdrawal, the main difference being no sea and no air force. I met all the C.O.s and some other Officers, including the acting C.O. of the 2/5 R.G.R., who had taken over from our Brigade Commander and had been in my Company at Sandhurst.

Shortly after my return to Brigade Headquarters the I.O. returned with a pipe, which he had got from a Burmese Inspector of Police, and a sack of raw leaf tobacco, which came from some Buddhist priests. The Brigade Commander, who already wore an Inspector of Police topee, sent the pipe to the Field Ambulance to be disinfected and I soaked the tobacco (some of it) in a mixture of ration rum and sugar and then it was dried on an Army blanket. The results? Well it was strong and worth at least 100 rupees an ounce!

Sometime during the evening, our Divisional Liaison Officer arrived to hand over orders for our withdrawal on the 22nd April.

Divisional Headquarters were to withdraw on the 21st April.

A Brigade Conference was ordered at about 1800 hours on the 20th. We met the Chinese C.O. again and found that he had conjunctivitis. Someone found a spare pair of dark glasses, which the C.O. wore, even at night. Sung, we were told, was his name.

This Battalion of the Chinese 5th Army (2/187 Regiment) had a British Officer attached as a Liaison Officer and Interpreter. This one had been in the Chinese Customs and was most useful. He was, in many ways, an extraordinary man. He appeared to have a never-ending supply of paperback books and a camp bed. During any form of battle he opened up his bed close to his Battalion and started to read.

During the time that the 2/187 Regt. was under command I got to know their C.O. and soon liked him and a number of his Officers very much indeed.

The withdrawal was ordered to start at 1800 hours on 22nd April, which was after darkness fell. During the night 21/22 April we found that the wireless we had was unable to contact Divisional Headquarters. In the early days the wireless always failed at night — we got used to it! We did not know how far we had to retreat, we only knew the route we were to take and we were told that we should receive orders. Before Div. H.Q. left I was given the key of the jail and told to throw it over the gates before leaving myself. This I did and shouted out in Urdu that I had done so. I hope they found the key.

We left Taungdwingyi at about 1800 hours. We passed through the Rear Guard which consisted of a Brigade of Burma Division (BURDIV). The Brigade Commander was from a Gurkha Regiment, so too was his Brigade Major an old friend of mine. We gave them what news we had and then continued on our way.

We arrived at Myothit at about 0400 hours and, after a rapid check to locate the Headquarters of our Units, I lay down in the village street to get a little sleep. I woke up and found that something had decided to use my chest as a camp bed. I found it to be a very friendly Burmese cat. We became friends before it walked off.

The village was full of stray pigs, which was too much for our Chinese friends, and soon we had the choice of being shot by a Chinese marksman or being charged by a wounded pig! Other marksmen were taking pot shots at pigeons and life became very dangerous. The Brigadier sent for the C.O. of 2/187 and told him that this indiscriminate shooting would stop at once. We had no more trouble of that sort.

The Chinese we met would eat anything that moved. Everything was thrown into a large brass pot and most of it had undergone the minimum of cleaning; so, if one asked to take a meal with our 'comrades-in-arms', one hoped that one would not pull out a half-cleaned snake! I managed to find an excuse at meal times. I was getting to know our Chinese and found them to be very honest children, who shot first and challenged after. Every evening they listened to their leader, Chiang Kai-shek, and received orders.

They said they were very happy as soldiers, as they would die with full stomachs and a few Chinese dollars, whereas in civil life they would starve without any money. Life meant very little to them, either their own or other people's. The following story will illustrate this.

Three sentries were guarding a ration dump, one British, one Gurkha and one Chinese. A Burman was hanging about with the obvious intent of stealing something. The B.O.R. told him to 'push off', which he did not do. When he got to the Chinese sentry, the sentry shot him. The other two sentries asked him why he had done this, he replied, 'You told him that it was time to go away. He did not do so, I thought that it was time he learnt a lesson.'

We remained at Myothit for the hours of daylight and then withdrew to Mahlaing at 1800 hours, which we reached at 1130 hours on 24th April, 1942. Mahlaing proved to be an unhealthy spot! Bde. H.Q. was located in a large Burmese house and compound. I decided to make use of the lavatory, which was a shed with open slots in the house compound. I had hardly got there when I spotted two Burmans stalking me. I shouted to them to 'clear off'. They did so, but I spotted them again — a bit nearer this time. I drew my revolver and put it through the slots, shouting out as I did so that I would shoot them if they came any nearer. I reported the incident to the Brigade Commander.

Shortly after dark a Gurkha Patrol brought in five Burmans, who had been seen setting the ammunition dump on fire. I reported the matter to the Brigadier, who was talking to one of the C.O.s. When he had read the message which the patrol brought with them, he ordered the Fifth Columnists to be shot. I wondered what I could do about it and who should provide the 'shooting party'. I could think of nothing I had ever learnt which laid down the procedure for shooting 'Fifth Columnists'.

However, just at that moment the C.O. of the 2/187 Regt. came along and asked what the trouble was, I told him and he replied, 'Of course they must be shot. I will supply the men to do it under the command of one of my Majors. The only condition is that you will attend the execution.'

My orders were to see that the men were shot, so I replied that I would be there and that the Chinese Major would command his own men. The Chinese very soon arrived and marched the 'Fifth Columnists' off towards the fire they had started, so that any of their friends who were 'lying-up' could see what could happen to them.

I was still wondering what the procedure would be when the Chinese Major said, 'Will this spot do?'

I said yes. He gave some order and a Chinese stepped forward and shot each of the culprits in turn. The Major then turned to me, shook hands and said, 'Goodnight! A job well done.' and marched off.

This will also illustrate how much the Chinese valued life.

Early the next morning Bde. H.Q. moved to a more salubrious position in a railway cutting. The Brigade from the Burma Division moved to Mahlaing.

That evening, 25th April, sudden orders were received to move to Kyaukse. We had just received a Humber Saloon, left by the Governor.

Later in the evening of 24th April, Colonel Sung arrived at Bde. H.Q. and told us that he had received orders to rejoin their 5th Army and that he would be away very early the next morning. He also added that he was considering disobeying the order. I asked him why and he replied, 'Because you have cheese in your rations'.

We had a good laugh and he said his goodbyes. I was intrigued by the number of Cadet Officers that the 2/187 Regt. appeared to have and that none of them carried any weapons. I was told that these young men, before they could become Commissioned Officers, must first prove themselves in battle. I also got a request from one of the Regiment's Majors that he and some Cadets should have the opportunity of riding on a tank, if possible in battle. A Tank Commander said he would arrange for them to accompany a Tank Patrol, which he did, and everybody was happy!

The Chinese, who had already known war before Burma, were first-class diggers. They managed to dig-in and then to dig an alternate position by the time we had dug one. They carried all their equipment, including medium machine guns, slung on a bamboo pole between two men. If they had any mechanised transport in a Regiment it carried the medical stores, doctor and a nurse. The 2/187 had no vehicles.

The Burma–Thai border.

The Burma–Thai border.

1/7th of G.R. Bo's.

An Officer's home.

Brigade Commander fishing at Manipur.

Bath time.

A mascot.

Sittang River where many lost their lives after the bridge was blown.

At Taungdwingyi, planned in 1942 as a "final stand".

Pynging.

2nd Royal Tanks ferrying.

48th Bde., Mawlaik.

Last of the tanks at Sweygein.

3″ mortar to range.

Refugees from Imphal.

Chapter 13

The Battle of Kyaukse
Withdrawal to Myinu

During the very early hours of 26th April, the Brigadier and I left the Brigade to carry out a recce to Kyaukse in our newly acquired Humber car. We soon found ourselves in the midst of the retreating Chinese 5th Army, which can best be described as an armed rabble, some of whom had terrible wounds. We decided that the only thing to do was to drive as fast as we could. I was driving and I put my foot down!

I was now to find out that my Commander was a great soldier with an uncanny 'eye for ground', who could often predict the type of ground behind a hill. While I was driving through the Chinese, the Bde. Commander was making a careful study of the ground which consisted of never-ending small fields, across a road ditch and separated on all sides by small banks which would stop any vehicle from crossing the land. The Bde. Commander spotted the only place where it would be possible to deploy artillery. We had no gridded maps and only a map of Burma given to me by a Forest Officer. However, the Brigadier made a very accurate estimate of the distance of the track from Kyaukse.

We were able to make our recce before the Brigade arrived followed by Div. H.Q. We heard that General Stillwell (Vinegar Jo!) of the U.S. Forces and Commander of the Chinese in Burma, had his headquarters in Kyaukse, so the Brigadier reported to the General and returned with a somewhat jaundiced opinion of the American.

Bde. H.Q. were located in an empty Buddhist Monastery behind the 1/7th G.R. and bounded on the right flank by a small stream, which gave a member

81

of the Defence Platoon a lot of pleasure as he had a fishing line. In fact, this man, a G.O.R., fished throughout the forthcoming battle and I think that he caught a 'sardine or two!' The south side of our position was protected by a much larger stream but not an anti-tank obstacle. The right flank had a deep ditch, which was an obstacle to tanks. Both water courses had important bridges which carried two roads to Kyaukse. The larger stream allowed us all to have a good wash and we all appreciated the chance to do so.

The 27th April was spent sending out Patrols to find out what the enemy was doing, also a number of recces were undertaken and several small hills close to Kyaukse were occupied or used as Observation Posts. The Monastery appeared to have a number of Tuktu lizards. The men had their own name for these creatures and said if they made their peculiar call six times we should be ordered to withdraw. The Monastery creatures stuck at five times during the 27th (changed to six on the 28th!).

Divisional H.Q. moved out of Kyaukse and 7th Hussars came under command. A battery of 25 Pdr. Guns were sent up to Kyaukse to support the Brigade and it was then that the Brigade Commander's knowledge of ground proved so vital. He told the Battery Commander where he expected the enemy to deploy his guns. Our Gunners had a map and the Brigadier was able to pick the exact spot. During some Patrol one of our men had been captured and kept by the Japanese with their forward troops. This man managed to escape and confirm that when our guns opened fire they landed their shells on top of an enemy gun or guns. Our field battery came from the 1st Indian Field Regiment and were commanded by absolutely first-class Indian Officers, one of whom became a great friend of mine. He was one of the last Indian Officers I met just before leaving India for good after the war was over.

At about 2100 hours the enemy made contact and we were shelled very hard. Earlier in the evening, before darkness fell, the Brigadier paid a visit to a post near the main road bridge. While he was there a Japanese patrol came down the road and the Brigadier manned the post's light machine gun and opened fire. He missed his target who dived into the ditch. According to the Brigadier, who was still laughing on arrival at his Headquarters, the language used by our post was worth hearing!

Shelling went on for most of the night and it was then that our Gunners opened fire and landed on top of the enemy guns. The enemy made one or two attempts to enter Kyaukse but failed to make any progress.

As dawn on the 29th April broke, shelling increased and more attacks came in, but all were driven back. The battle went on all day and the tanks were ordered to recce on our right flank and ordered to pay special attention to a small wood. This meant that they had to cross a bridge across the small stream I have mentioned, which was an anti-tank obstacle. The 7th Hussar Commander was told how long he was to be out and also that the bridge across the stream was being prepared for demolition by our Sappers. The question of Commander of the Bridge, who would order the Sappers to blow their charges, was soon settled — it was me.

I went over to the bridge, put the staff car behind a house and waited for the tanks to come back. The Brigade Commander came up to see all was in order and while he was there the main road bridge was blown up. In the meantime the enemy appeared to have called a halt, as there was no sign of him on our front and also no firing except by his guns.

It had been arranged that after I had been given the order to blow the bridge across the ditch I should go back to 63 Brigade, which was in position acting as rear guard somewhere down the road, and that I should give their Commander such information as I had.

It was while I was waiting for the tanks to return that I witnessed an incident which illustrated the influence a man could have over others. The Chaplain of the 7th Armoured Brigade, I had met in the hospital at Pegu, had a large station wagon as transport. On the sides of this vehicle was the word 'Chaplain' in large letters. Firing had started again in the area of the main road. The Chaplain's vehicle was seen speeding along the road towards the firing where some of the 7th Hussar tanks were being deployed.

I heard a Gurkha remark to another, 'The Padre Sahib had gone forward, all will be well.'

I think that by now everyone had heard that the very brave Chaplain had stayed behind at Pegu after the enemy had taken over, found as many dead as he and the few men he had with him could, and buried them in shallow graves. The Chaplain and his noble squad then proceeded to march over twenty miles. By this time the Chaplain's boots had given out, so he rejoined in his stockinged feet. For this brave act the Chaplain was awarded the D.S.O.

He became a kind of legend and was much admired by all ranks of all religions.

I have always hoped that those who were with the Brigadier and myself when we were ambushed on 6th April were found and buried. I heard that they were, but I was unable to confirm the information.

The two tanks returned from their task and reported that they had seen no signs of any enemy on our right flank. I asked their C.O. if all his troops were now back over the bridge and if there were any more of our troops across the stream on the enemy front. He confirmed that all his tanks were across the bridge and that none of our troops had been left behind. I then told my 'force', consisting of my Batman, Driver and a handful of Sappers, to take cover and ordered the Sapper Officer to blow the bridge, which he did.

The enemy in the meantime were somewhat half-heartedly carrying on their fire on our left flank.

As soon as the bridge had been blown and I had seen the Sappers get into their truck and withdraw, we got into our transport and proceeded to contact 63 Bde. H.Q.

The enemy guns now started to shell the road but nothing was hit.

We arrived at 63 Bde. H.Q. and reported to the Acting Brigade Commander. I met no-one I knew and, after we had all had something to eat and had arranged for some food for our Brigadier and his party, we left to meet the Brigadier.

He soon came down the road and we went to 63 Bde. H.Q. once again. After a very rapid meal we were on our way back towards Mandalay, not knowing where Div. H.Q. was located as the wireless was up to its old tricks.

48 Bde. withdrew at about 1800 hours on 29th April and so the battle of Kyaukse was over and I was full of admiration for our Brigade Commander.

During our occupation of Kyaukse a number of enemy air squadrons passed overhead, but only one 'Zero' took any interest in us. The aircraft used to arrive at about 0900 hours, have a look round, then at 09.30 hours drop a couple of light bombs, open up with its machine guns and then fly home.

Just after the 'Zero' had paid its visit, one of our Hurricanes would turn up, the only one in Burma we were told. Where it came from and who the pilot was we never knew but we liked to see it. We never found out if the 'Zero' and our Hurricane ever met. We saw our Hurricane after Kyaukse, but not the Zero, so perhaps?

We moved down the road and soon found that it was full of troops from Depots, etc., Burmans getting away from the advancing Japanese and Indian refugees. We eventually found the Div. H.Q. sign and reported the arrival of 48 Bde. We were given our orders which were to occupy Myinu, a small town at the junction of the Irrawaddy and Chindwin rivers.

Chapter 14

Myinu

We crossed the Irrawaddy by the Ava bridge, then turned left and took the road down the river Irawaddy left bank and reached Myinu about 0300 hours.

Bde. H.Q. was in a small medical centre with a lot of useful things, such as syringes, lying about. These we collected and gave to our Field Ambulance. While I was deciding where to have a sleep, our I.O. said, 'I think you had better have a look at an old Indian I have found in an out-house. He is in a terrible mess'.

I went along and found an elderly Indian covered in cuts from a Burmese Dar. It looked as if someone had inflicted 'death by a thousand cuts', but the old man was still alive, in spite of the fact that most of his wounds had become septic. I sent the I.O. off to find an M.O. while I stayed with the victim, who died before the M.O. arrived.

All our Battalions were soon connected to Bde. H.Q. by telephone and reported 'all's well'. I realised that I was now getting about two and a half hours sleep in seventy-two hours, so decided to have a short nap before dawn. I had hardly got my head down before firing (L.M.G.) started in the direction of the river Irrawaddy. I got into a jeep and went off to find out what I could. I found a Royal Marine Commando Detachment were sinking some Irrawaddy River Steamers. They told me that the river was very shallow and could be crossed with ease. I went on and contacted the C.O.s of our Battalions and told them about the Royal Marines.

We spent the next few days having a wash and resting. The Brigadier and I had a look at the country to the north and found the main Myinu hospital and, to our amazement, on the pavement outside the hospital were four stretchers on which were four wounded Officers who told us that they had been told that ambulances would pick them up, on their return from Monywa.

The wounded were given food and water, they had been there for twenty-four hours. We arranged for them to be looked after by an M.O. but also had to tell them that without an ambulance they could not be moved. We expected to get orders to cut across country and had no means of carrying any badly wounded.

On 1st May the 1/4th G.R. were ordered to Monywa under the command of Burdiv and we received a warning order that the remainder of the Brigade would also move to Burdiv.

On May 2nd we received orders to join Burdiv by train. The train never arrived and later that day we received a message. This message thanked us for all that the Brigade had done and added that we were now completely cut-off. If we could manage it, we were told to cross country and join 17 Div. as best we could.

We set off for a place called Saduang which was on the main road to Mandalay. We had only proceeded a short way towards a bullock cart track, which ran close to the river Yu, when the enemy air force flew over in strength. They did not take any apparent interest in us, but we heard explosions away to our rear.

However, it was considered wise to get under the cover of a small wood. Several enemy squadrons flew overhead, but we were not bombed or machine gunned.

To amuse myself I decided to 'dowse' for water and cut a likely-looking twig from a tree. Armed with my twig I walked up and down, much to the amusement of my brother Officers. One of the men asked me what I was doing and I told him, 'looking for water'. Then to the amusement of us all we saw that several men had cut twigs and had joined in the search, aided on by many Gurkha remarks and leg-pulling.

After a while the enemy air activity died down and we continued our march up the dusty, rough track. At about 1500 hours the Brigadier called a halt and told everyone to have a meal and rest till dark.

The Brigade enjoyed a wash in the river Yu and the cooks got some sort of meal ready. When three men (Burmans) approached Bde. H.Q. they were met by our I.O., who reported to me that they would like to have a word with the Officer in Charge. I told the Brigadier and he said that he would see them.

One of the men from the village said that he was a Police Officer in the Burma Police who had been told to return to his home. He then said that it would give everyone in his village much pleasure if we would allow them to cook an evening meal for the Officers if we would give him the numbers. There were not many of us, so we included the three Clerks that we had.

I remembered that I had acquired a jelly square which I thought would add to the meal. What container should be used to melt the square and allow the jelly to set was the next problem. However, we soon decided to use a mule's nose bag, which could be hung from a tree in the hope that it would cool and the jelly would set. It did its best, but was only half set when we were ready for our pudding!

Our new friend turned up just after dark with a number of men from the village carrying an array of pots. They had cooked a delicious curry of chicken with vegetables, for which they would take nothing in the way of payment. We managed to obtain the policeman's name and rank and also the name of the village, which was given to an European Police Officer of the Burma Police, some weeks later.

One of the Bde. H.Q. jeeps had lost a back tyre. This jeep carried office equipment and was driven by one of our British Clerks. As the road we were using was full of ruts and holes the jeep often took over and decided its own route. Amusing to watch but very tiring for the driver.

As we approached Sadaung, the Brigadier ordered the Bde. to halt and occupy firing positions.

As far as we knew we were completely cut-off, so we expected Sadaung to be occupied by the enemy. The Bde. Commander then said that he and I would go forward and find out what we could. We thought that we heard men talking in Urdu. The Brigadier ordered me to stay where I was and cover him, while he tried to get a bit nearer. When he got back he said that he was certain that there were no enemy in Saduang, so we would go on and occupy the place. When we got there at 0200 hours, we found it occupied by our Supply Officer and his men, who somehow produced a mug of tea for all at Bde. H.Q. and some bread and cheese. The Supply Officer told us that he had seen no signs of the enemy since coming across the Irrawaddy, but that he had lost his Havildar and some men, who he feared were by now prisoners of war or dead.

Shortly after our arrival we heard the sounds of marching feet coming up the main road. I went forward with a few men and got into the road ditch while the 'marchers' came on. To our delight it was the missing Havildar, Raugupatti and the Supply Section men. I asked Raugupatti why they were making such a noise. He replied that he had told his men to do their best to make the enemy think they were a large column!

What remained of the night passed without incident and early the next day orders given to carry on up the main road and report to 17 Div. H.Q.

The enemy air force was fairly active with targets we could not see and one or two fighters were using their machine guns, again we could not see any targets.

The Brigade took up position on the outskirts of Ye-U but had been there only a short time when we received orders to move on to Ping Yein. Again the Brigade took up defensive positions on the outskirts and I was ordered to report to Div. H.Q. for orders. I was told to take a Platoon with me and deploy them wherever I considered necessary. I left this Platoon, under the command of a Naik (Corporal), a mile or so short of Div. H.Q. and regret to say that when I returned for them an hour or two later there was no trace of them. The Naik in Command decided that I was lost and withdrew the Platoon without orders.

At Div. H.Q. I was told that a canal ran along the south-west boundary of the Ping Yein area and that was where the Brigade was to form a defensive position. I was also told that a Battalion of J.A.T.S. from Burdiv was somewhere in our area and that they would be under command of 48 Bde. I found the C.O. of this Battalion on the road near his H.Q. truck. The Battalion, vastly under-strength like our Battalions, was deployed in the fields round about. I had taken a Liaison Officer with me and sent him back to Bde. H.Q. with a message, then went on to look at our area.

Just after I had contacted the Jat Bn.Co., our Supply Officer turned up and presented me with a side of bacon and my serious preoccupation was to keep the bacon out of the sun.

Shortly after this wonderful event, an enemy fighter aircraft swooped down at the C.O. and myself. We dived for cover under the truck and instinct made me choose the shade, so the bacon was saved and so were we!

We had one other fighter attack on us, after which the enemy, luckily, must have thought that we were not worthwhile.

After the second attack I went back to my Platoon and to report to the Brigade Commander. I found that the Platoon was not in the position I had given it so I went on to Bde. H.Q. I then led the Brigade to its new location and handed over the bacon to our cook, Sam. Sam was a Madrasi who we had somehow acquired in Burma. He was a great character and became very attached to us all and we to him.

The Brigadier and I decided that one of the things we would like at the moment was a tin each of apricots and we told our Supply Officer. This Officer could find anything, anywhere! Off he went and soon returned with a couple of tins. The Brigadier uttered his favourite expression which was 'WAH!' and said that we would enjoy our tinned apricots while sitting in the canal. We went for our bathe and found that we had no tin opener; however, with the aid of the kukri I carried, we got the tins opened only to find that they contained apricot jam! We had long ago lost our Mess knives and forks, etc., but had our own make, made by the men from bamboo. We even had something which resembled a spoon. Everyone carried their own set.

After our wash we went back to Bde. H.Q. and waited for orders. After a peaceful night we spent another day in our position, when orders were received to send out a strong fighting patrol, with a party of Officers, who under a Sapper Officer were engaged with activities designed to worry the enemy. They called themselves the 'Bush Wackers' and were the forerunners of a well-known force of the future.

Each Battalion was ordered to supply approximately (of Gurkhas) one Section and the Patrol was under the Command of a first-class Officer, an old friend of mine, a Major in the 7th G.R. and his small H.Q. staff. This again, was the forerunner of our Commando Platoons which were organised and equipped later.

This fighting patrol left during the afternoon and crossed the River Chindwin.

Later that same evening (May 5th) I was sent to Div. H.Q. to find out the situation. It was then that I saw what a mess refugees could make of a place. Ping Yein had a large number of refugees, some sick, some dead and all in a bad way.

While I was talking to the General the enemy attacked. They did not do much damage or get very far and Div. H.Q. survived without a scar. I thought that I should get back to Bde. H.Q. as soon as possible.

On the way I ran into a complete rabble of L. of C. troops, all running — they knew not where. I called over a young Sikh soldier and asked him why he was running and where to. This young man replied. 'The enemy have attacked so I joined the rest of my friends.'

I told him it was only an enemy Jitter Party who had achieved their object of frightening our soldiers and the refugees. I also told him to walk away, if he must, as running merely spread panic. He went off, quite happy and walking.

I got to Bde. and told the story of the attack on Div. H.Q. and that there were no casualties. I also gave the news that we should withdraw, again, the next day.

Chapter 15

Sweygein

The 1/4 G.R. rejoined the Brigade and we were once again a Brigade so far as Battalions were concerned, but not in strength or weapons.

That night (5/6 May) the enemy made no further attacks and all was quiet and we wondered what he was doing.

Our Patrols reported that there were no signs of the enemy.

On 6th May, we received orders to withdraw to Sweygein and that 9th Jats would be under command. We arrived at Sweygein during the early evening. Here we found all that was left of 17 Div., L. of C. Troops and 7th Armoured Brigade.

As I was walking along, a young Officer greeted me with the remark, 'Good evening, Sir, would you like a drink?'

I asked him where he had managed to obtain anything in the nature of a drink and he replied that some Armoured Brigade details had been in Rangoon before the final evacuation and that I could have anything I wished! I made my choice and got it. We also learnt that no vehicles could proceed any further and that it was the intention to burn the tanks.

Sweygein consisted of an amphitheatre with high cliffs, both north and south and the Chindwin on our right flank.

On the north side the only exit was by a narrow and steep path, little better than a goat track.

Our orders were to defend the withdrawal, so our troops were deployed in battle positions and we waited for the enemy to attack. The tanks were set on fire and we met the K.O.Y.L.I. and Duke of Wellington's Regiment or what was left of them. Both had suffered very heavy casualties.

Just after dark we heard sounds of battle on the cliffs to the south but could not see what was taking place. We hoped that it was an attack by our Commando Patrol. We learnt later that our 'hopes' were correct. The Commando Platoon had found the Japanese Officers having dinner under full lights and sitting at table. They 'shot-up' the enemy and withdrew across the Chindwin as they had no idea of what happened beyond the Officers' Mess, and had no maps.

Enemy firing, including mortar fire, plus some shelling continued all that night and increased after daylight.

The battle went on all day (8th May) but the enemy hit nothing and we had no casualties.

In the meantime, our troops were slowly moving up the hill track and we received orders to evacuate our positions and withdraw by the same and only track.

Firing started to increase and the Brigadier ordered me to go forward to find out what was happening. I went to see 1/7 G.R. and most of the firing was on their front.

On the cliff face opposite the 1/7 G.R. a sturdy-looking tree was growing. While I was talking to the C.O., to our amazement we saw a Japanese sniper jump off the top of the cliff and land in the tree and prepare to start sniping. A detachment of Gunners, who were manning a Bofors anti-aircraft gun, also saw the sniper and opened fire. After three rounds there was no tree and no sniper.

After a further look round I got into my jeep and returned to Bde. H.Q.

During the whole battle Sam, our cook, took no notice of enemy shells or mortar bombs and carried up cups of tea. I never saw Sam worried about anything.

Our orders were to start withdrawal at 1900 hours. We did not get away until 0400 hours on 9th May, owing to a completely blocked track. If men sat down, they fell asleep, thus adding to the chaos. The I.O. and myself moved up the track and saw the situation for ourselves. I found myself falling asleep on my feet!

Just before dark I pushed my jeep into a small pond which was located in some quick sands and watched it sink very slowly. I removed the ignition key, which I still have in a collection of old keys.

Eventually the track cleared and we were able to move, but as I said it was not until 0400 hours.

When we were clear of the track we found some of our transport had been driven round by the main road and was waiting for us.

During the evacuation of Europeans and others from Burma many pets had left home with their owners and some had wandered off on their own. Shortly after I found a Bde. jeep and we had started, I came across a Golden Labrador looking very lost. I told it to get into my vehicle, which it did, and soon fell asleep. This dog stayed with me long enough to eat a ration biscuit, then it wandered off and I did not see it again.

We had orders to withdraw to the River Chindwin and embark on a river steamer for Kalewa.

The enemy made no attempt to follow-up and we disembarked at Kalewa at about midday. We learnt that the Bde., which now consisted of six Battalions and had a strength of some 400 all ranks, would leave Kalewa after dark and travel by steamer to Sittaung. From Sittaung our route was by track and road to Imphal in Manipur State in Assam.

We told the ship's Captain that we must halt until daylight in order to pick up our Commando Platoon.

This was suitable as navigation of the Chindwin was not possible after dark without lights. The Brigade Commander was given a cabin and the rest of the Brigade settled down on deck. In the ship's lounge we found a wireless set which worked, so we heard the news and more about the situation in Burma than we knew ourselves. We were given the news that all was lost in Burma and that the Army was now cut off and there was little hope of anyone escaping. This news was greeted with loud cheers!

The remainder of our Division, L. of C. troops and other Units was withdrawing on the road from Kalewa to Assam and had to march through the Kabaw valley, notorious for malaria. This malaria was often the cerebral type and I am afraid that many men died.

We had anchored in midstream and waited.

At last we heard movement on the right bank but had no idea if it was our Commando Platoon or the enemy. We were to learn that it was our Commando Platoon and that they were doubtful about our identity. The Commander of the Platoon was drowned in the Chindwin.

Dawn broke on May 11th, without us knowing what had happened to the Platoon, so it was decided that we should continue upstream and tie up at Mawlaik.

We left our anchorage as soon as navigation became possible and arrived at Mawlaik during the morning. The Brigadier issued orders that some members of the Bde. Staff, i.e. myself, I.O. and Signal Officer, would go ashore with him and a small escort. The rest of the Brigade would remain on the ship.

We were unable to get any trace of the Commando Platoon and we saw no-one to question about their whereabouts.

We had a good look round and saw nothing except empty houses. We found the Mawlaik Club and went in.

In the Club we found a silver cup presented for some golf competition and a book containing prints of duck, also one hen's egg. I put the silver cup and book into my haversack and somebody carried the egg, which the Brigadier enjoyed later.

We dropped anchor again for the night and reached Sittaung at 10.00 a.m. the next morning. The whole Brigade was ordered to disembark and to take up defence positions.

Before we left Kalewa I was given three bags, each containing 1,000 Queen Victoria silver rupees, with orders to distribute 1,000 to the refugees who were collecting at a village a little further from Sittaung, which I think was called Paungbyin.

The I.O. and one other Officer set sail and gave the money to the Indians and others. The ship then came back to Sittaung and the two Officers rejoined Bde. H.Q. Somebody carried the remaining two bags of money.

The Bde. Transport Officer found a Bombay and Burma Company elephant with its mahout and two bicycles.

We had the money to pay for our needs and now had some transport to carry the money, two of our men who had cholera and some other odds and ends.

The mahout said that his elephant had recently got over being MUSK and could be a little bit bolshy at times. Our only two mortars were loaded on to the elephant and the transport set off an hour or so before the rest of us, who started on the next phase of the withdrawal at 1630 hours, leaving one Battalion to hold the track to Ya-Nan on the banks of the river Yu, about thirty-six miles away. The road was through thick jungle rising 2,000 feet to a pass.

On the way we met a young Officer who had been sent to locate the Bde. and report back to 17 Div. H.Q. He told the Brigadier that at the pass was a Rest house which drew its water from a well and a small stream and that it would be possible to fill our water bottles from these two sources.

On the march we thought we heard Japs calling to each other and making odd noises, such as their Jitter Parties often made. However, we soon decided that it was a party of Gibbon monkeys.

When we reached the pass it was soon realised that it would take a good few hours to fill water bottles, and the water both in the well and from the stream was highly contaminated with the bodies of dead refugees, most of whom had died of cholera. The reader can imagine the smell.

The Brigadier ordered the Bde. to march on until we found a healthier spot.

Not long after we had left the pass but were still on the Sittaung side, dawn broke. We found our transport sitting down on the track. I told the Bde. Transport Officer to get the elephant out of the way. He explained that this beast would only walk a maximum of twelve miles, then it demanded a rest. I suggested a fire under its tail might help! The mahout said that it behaved like this because of Musk and it would soon start again, so we left it and it turned up at our next position soon after we got there.

We soon found ourselves on the other side of the hills looking down on the Yu river far below us. The Brigadier ordered an hour's halt which was very welcome after our very hot and waterless march.

While we were resting Havildar Raugupatti came along, as cheerful as ever, and said that he had a water bottle of milk and there was just enough for the Officers.

When we got to Ya-Nan the Brigadier allocated areas, then the Brigade fell into the Yu river like a herd of cattle! It was wonderful to just sit in the cool, fast water and just absorb moisture.

The Divisional Liaison officer for our Brigade arrived and said that the Brigade would remain where it was until May 15th (it was now May 13th) when it would receive fresh orders. The Liaison Officer did a great job throughout the Retreat and never failed to get through to us.

We had a good night's rest in what we thought was Shangri-La. So did the elephant, who found plenty of good shrubs to eat. The mahout said that he would like to get back to the Chindwin as soon as he could. We thanked him and gave him a bag of 1,000 rupees for his help. He went off a happy man.

During the 14th May the Battalion that had been left at Sittaung arrived, also an American jeep and an American aircraft.

Three American Officers told us they had come forward to get news of General Stillwell, who had been missing for some days. We had not seen a sign of him and were unable to help. We were told that the aircraft had some fresh food aboard and also a case of whisky for the General. We tried everything we could to make those on the aircraft drop their load on us. But our efforts met with no success! We heard later that the General was safe.

After a further swim we were ready to move again. I went round the Battalions to see how they all were and found them to be in good heart.

When I got to 1/4 G.R. they were having a meal of sorts at Bn.H.Q. Their C.O. said he wished to make a complaint, which he did with a twinkle in his eye.

The Battalion held a position across the river guarding the bridge. Battalion

The Battalion held a position across the river guarding the bridge. Battalion H.Q. was in a field which had been used by elephants. The C.O. had a tin plate and mug in front of him, each sitting on an elephant dropping. His complaint was, he expected Brigade to supply better tables!

We learnt later that the Nips were shooting refugees and others, who were in possession of Queen Victoria rupees. The rupees had been declared as obsolete and anyone who was found with one was declared a 'collaborator with the British'.

When we reached Manipur no-one would accept the rupees we had, neither would any Bank or Treasury in India. We had them melted down and made into silver cigarette cases and gave them to every officer in Bde. and Div. Headquarters, who was still alive. Mine, alas, fell into enemy hands when we had to evacuate Tiddim, several months later.

Chapter 16

Manipur

We left Ya-Nan that night and after a very short march reached Tamu an hour and a half later and spent the 16th May watching the road and refugees.

By now we had received a few trucks and a jeep so we had transport for our remaining 3″ mortars, sick and the last bag of rupees.

We left Tamu in the middle of the night and set off for Lochao. At one halt I found a small green parrot which climbed on to my shoulder where it slept till the next halt. The Brigadier said that he considered putting me under arrest for being improperly dressed!

During the last stages of this march a very smart-looking Corporal of Seaforth Highlanders met us and reported that he had been ordered to report to Bde. H.Q. and lead us into the area allocated to the Brigade. I told him that this was Bde. H.Q. and the Brigade Commander was beside me. He saluted and gave us a queer look!

We were filthy and battle weary and delighted to see the Corporal. I asked him where he came from and he replied — Elgin. I told him that I came from the same place. I think that I am right in saying that this man won the first M.M. of the Regiment some months later while on Fighting Patrol to the Yu river.

The Battalion of Seaforth Highlanders were holding the pass above Lochao and we had been given some straw houses (bashas) which were close by. The men had a different name for the place, which was full of dead and dying refugees, others with dysentery. No attempt had been made by these wretched people to dig any latrines or get rid of their dead. It was an appalling mess. However, we were not too close and appreciated our huts, as the early rains of the monsoon had arrived.

During the withdrawal no-one had thought of the change in the time zone and we found ourselves going to bed and getting up in the morning at different times to the Seaforths, until our Signals Officer set his watch to the right time.

We spent two days at this desirable place and left on the 18th May for a march of seventeen and a half miles by hill road, which had a thick covering of mud and slush due to the heavy showers.

Transport met us about ten miles from Palel which we reached at 1930 hours and halted under cover for a meal.

The Brigadier had gone ahead to report to 17 Div. H.Q. and to find out where we had to go. We left Palel early in the night (18th May) and after an uneventful journey arrived at Imphal.

The Brigadier had selected Battalion areas and located Bde. H.Q. in a great spot, in fact it was a truly 'desirable property'.

The next day we had a look round our area, which consisted of a deserted village. The houses were thatched and very often used to house carts and farm implements, probably also some cattle and goats. Near by was a large, open, grass-covered field with a small hill at the centre.

Many houses had a pond, some quite large, in the compound which was home to muddy-looking fish which the men enjoyed. Everywhere bamboo grew in profusion. There were clumps of bamboo and hedges of bamboo. This 'tree' was to become our friend and was used for our training. Imphal was about two miles away, where the bazaar had been burnt down as the result of enemy air raids and many of the tradespeople had run away.

17 Div. H.Q. was located at Imphal, which in peace time was an important Government centre for Manipur State and was about eighty miles from Railhead, a place called Dimapur. The road to Dimapur was a narrow hill road and unsuitable for the maintenance of fighting troops. It was capable of use by light transport and soon steps had been taken to make this a very good road with the help of local planters and their coolies, also the local tribes mostly Nagas and Kukies and others, both men and women. What a splendid job these people did under the guidance of our Sappers.

About three-quarters of the way down the hill road towards Dimapur was an administrative centre called Kohima, which was to be the scene of very severe fighting and many acts of supreme bravery.

63 Bde. was located in the Kohima area with the 1/3 G.R. holding a spur to the north through which an important track to Burma passed.

We all thought that we should be given good or better rations. However, we were told that we should still be on half-ration scales and got the same, soya link sausages, herrings in tomato sauce and no fresh vegetables. We had to put up with this for many weeks.

We heard that some kind ladies in Calcutta had adopted 17 Div. and had organised much-needed parcels of soap, razor blades, etc.; also other amenities such as footballs, wireless sets, dart boards and other games. To start with nothing arrived, they were all looted at the railway yards at Calcutta!

It was decided that a Composite Platoon under my command should pay the looters a visit and teach them a lesson. In the event this was cancelled and parcels started to get through. The postal arrangements were very poor, but soon improved and we learnt that many citations which had originated in Burma had been lost.

We soon had some amenities and something for the men to do in their spare time. Thank you, ladies, I only hope you knew the amount of pleasure you gave.

After we had settled in it was time to consider reorganisation of Bde. H.Q. and to talk about the lessons we had learnt.

One of the first priorities was to teach everyone to swim and to use local items to ferry equipment and stores over large rivers. The next was to get to know what could be made from bamboo and what obstacles it put in the way of attacking forces. It was also quite vital to ensure that Officers could talk to their men in the men's own language and not through a G.O.

All this was planned when reinforcements came up and we had some equipment and vital stores and after everyone had had some leave, as it had been decided the Div. would not be re-equipped in India, and would remain in Manipur.

At last the day came when we heard that the first stores would arrive. They arrived and turned out to be 'Poles — Mosquito' made of bamboo! But no nets came with the poles.

In the meantime we had been given a role to support 23 Ind. Div. and had to be prepared to go anywhere on the 23 Div. front.

The monsoon had by now broken in its full force and how it rained!

The Brigadier went off on leave and the remainder of us went off on orders of the Div. Commander. By now we had a full Brigade staff. The Brigadier had a brilliant idea that our Supply Officer should become Staff Captain. Other minor changes were made and Liaison Officers appointed.

The I.O. and Senior Signals Officer were unchanged and we became a team of young people with great confidence in our Commander and in the future of defeating the enemy. The part played by our Div. Commander in building up morale and a great spirit in his division was outstanding.

morale and a great spirit in his division was outstanding.

The Divisional sign was changed to a black cat with arched back and the Jap called us the '*Koeraaniko Bhutai*' which I think means Black Cat Formation.

When we (Staff Captain, I.O., Signals Officer and myself) reached Dimapur on leave, we found that we were all improperly dressed according to Army Regulations. However, there was nothing we could do about it as we had nothing else. While waiting for the train the next day, the sole of my shoe became unstuck. I had to ask a smart-looking Military Policeman if he had a knife and if so would he cut off the sole. I think that he considered putting me under arrest! I told him that I had worn these shoes since Rangoon and had nothing else.

We soon learnt that some bridge towards Gauhati had been damaged by monsoon floods and that the ferry was out of order: the train would take us a long way down the Brahmaputra and that we should spend most of the day on a river steamer on our way to Railhead, but would reach Calcutta that evening. We had a very cheerful journey. The Signals Officer and myself left for Madras the next day. I hoped to meet my wife, and my friend to catch a train for Ceylon to get married.

I met Joan at Madras where we spent the day before taking the night train to Ootacamund in the Nilgri hills, where Joan had taken a bungalow for herself and our son and had taken in her two cousins who had walked out of Burma with their two children. He was an Officer in the Burma Forest Service. I heard a lot about their walk out of Burma and how elephants helped the women and children under command of 'Elephant Bill' and Bandoola.

We had a grand leave together, playing golf and fishing. I paid a visit to the doctor who checked my old wounds and had a number of X-rays taken. These X-rays showed bits of shrapnel, which I was told would slowly work their way out. They have, except for the bits in my head, some of which have been removed from time to time by my doctor.

My left knee had several pieces of shrapnel in the joint and I was told that they would not worry me — they never have.

During my leave I was ordered to go to the Officer Producing Unit at Bangalore. Joan had decided to return to her Father at Hyderabad, and Bangalore was en route.

By now the 1942 Rebellion had started and trains did not move at night. This we did not know until we arrived at some station or other just before dark and were told that the train would go no further that night. Joan and I went up the platform in search of something to eat, having seen that all the windows in our carriage were locked and that my Bearer was inside with our son and Nanny.

When we knew that the carriage door was locked we went off. We got a meal and bought some food for Nanny and we found that there were no signs of trouble.

I must admit that looking after two women and a small baby was alarming and I slept with a loaded revolver. However, I need not have bothered as there was no noise or problems to bother about.

We moved off again the next day and got to Bangalore during the early afternoon in time to give my talk to the Cadets on Burma and the problems we faced. I stressed the points that Officers must be able to speak the language of their men, carry far less in the way of baggage and be really fit.

The only snag was that no trains would be running that night, so the Commandant and his wife kindly put us all up for the night and were most kind.

We were on our way next morning and as far as I can remember reached Castle Hill, our destination, that evening. I still had a few days of leave left which we spent at Castle Hill.

Time to set forth again soon came round and I found that trains would run at night. I said goodbye to my wife and son and boarded the train for Calcutta.

When I reported to Movement Control the next morning after arriving at Calcutta, I was told that there was no hope of getting to the war area for at least a week because of the backlog of troops and stores due to the Rebellion. I said a few words about my feelings and a voice said, 'You seem to be bit het-up, what's the trouble?'

I found an R.A.F. Wing-Commander behind me and I told him that I was Brigade Major of a Brigade, on leave and must get back to Manipur.

He told me to report to him the next morning at Dum-Dum Aerodrome and that he would fly me to Agatalla where he was Station Commander and he would arrange for my onward flight to Imphal. I told him that I had a case of gin with me and he replied, 'O.K. I have an empty Dakota.'

As we landed at Agatalla air raid Red was broadcast and I had the delightful sight of seeing the elephants, who were employed on the aerodrome, being put into slit trenches.

I made my way to the Officers' Mess which was located above the aerodrome. The Jap Air Force decided on another aerodrome and dropped their bombs there. At the Mess I found a young Officer of our Division and while we were talking, the 'All Clear' signal was given and the elephants left their slit trenches and resumed their work. We spent a comfortable night and the next day reported to the Station Commander who told us that a Lockheed Hudson aircraft would take me and the case of gin to Imphal, but that the other Officer would have to wait as the Lockheed was full of reinforcements.

The aircraft was very heavily loaded but we got away quite safely. Just after we had taken off the pilot called me and gave me a Bren gun with some full magazines and told me to stick it out of a window and be prepared to open fire, on his orders, on any attacking enemy fighters. He repeated that there was to be no firing without his direct order. The pilot told me that he had received a wireless message to say that a squadron of enemy fighters was spotted heading for, it was thought, Agatalla. They, however, did not worry us and were driven off by our fighters as they turned towards another R.A.F. aerodrome.

After we had landed at Imphal I made my way to Div. H.Q. and put through a telephone call to 48 Bde H.Q. and asked for some transport for myself and the case of gin. It soon arrived and I was back at H.Q. once again, where I found everyone had got back and were in good heart.

Due to what was to become known as the 1942 Rebellion, the Brigade was not re-equipped or fully reinforced until October.

The Division was made into a Light Division of two Infantry Brigades (48 and 63), a Support Battalion and two Recce Battalions, with jeep and ponies and mules. They did not remain as such for very long and reverted to useful Infantry Battalions.

During this period many conferences took place and the Blitz Formation, Harbouring Drill, swimming and British Officers' Language Classes were practised.

We started by saying 'to Mandalay without a mule' and tried out some light hand carts but soon gave them up as they became mud-bound.

We received orders that we had forty days to train before the Division was required to take part in an operation towards Tiddim and then on to Burma, in conjunction with a Special Force (Chindits).

During my short stay at Agatalla I had met two Gurkha Officers of my own Battalion who were now with the Chindits. I had a serious talk with them and gained the information that they were not very happy, as the Chindits were organised as Columns of mixed troops and might be under the command of a Column Commander who knew nothing about Gurkhas and could speak nothing but English.

I heard that one of the Column Commanders was an old friend from my Battalion of 2/2 G.R. I managed to have a few words with him as he was marching through Imphal and he was glad to have a brief word from someone who had been in Burma and met the Japs. I was able to see for myself what my two Gurkha Officer friends were worried about. My friend never returned from Burma and was drowned or killed while crossing the Irrawadday. I do not want to express any views about the Chindits, who did a very good job, but I have always felt that too many good men were wasted at a time when they were wanted in proper Divisions and not killed off or ravaged by malaria and other illness.

We had several visits from people who had made their names as botanists or had become known big game hunters. We learnt a lot of useful tips from them and discovered that many of the plants and shrubs that grew in the jungle were edible or quenched thirst. We also learnt that certain bamboo held water (of sorts) and others could be used for cooking rice.

We were, after a visit from the Corps Commander, getting a larger ration, some fresh vegetables and fish. The local inhabitants found that the Army were a useful source of income and reopened the Bazaar.

A Divisional Concert Party gave an excellent show and morale was rising. Our new Divisional R.A. Unit had been a Territorial Army Unit from Edinburgh with a number of Officers who had connections with firms in Bombay and Calcutta, some of whom I had met playing rugby.

The men of this Unit came from Edinburgh and the district close by. One of the Concert Party had been at Drama School when war was declared.

He took the part in the Concert Party of a very convincing girl. In his Field Regiment he was an Officer's Batman and one morning he decided to test his dress and make-up on his Officer.

He looked the part and called his Officer early one morning with a mug of tea. Rumour had it that the Officer concerned reported to the M.O. that he had developed jungle madness and must be evacuated as he had been called on by a beautiful young girl.

The Brigade Commander selected an area for all our Units to carry out Battalion Training and to start living hard. Bde. H.Q. carried out runs or P.T. every morning and all practised Harbouring and Blitz as well as jungle signals which had been evolved in order to cut out talking in action.

Before we left Imphal the Brigadier said that we should hold a 'Guest Night'. The Staff Captain was told to find something worthwhile to eat and drink — which he did! Sam, the cook, was thrilled and said he would produce menu cards. The last item on Sam's menu was 'Paddy Grass'. We were agog to know what this could be, but Sam would not give away his secret. When the savoury arrived it proved to be tinned asparagus! How or where our Staff Captain found such a thing, only he knew.

When we first took over our H.Q. we found some kittens, one of which became very tame and was named Hoskyns. She used to sleep with me and liked nothing better than to fight her brother through my mosquito net.

Canna grew in large clumps near our H.Q. so it was decided to dig them up and make a canna bed in a corner of the courtyard. We got hold of some manure and made the bed. To our delight, when the first canna came into flower it attracted a beautiful little bird called a honey bird. It arrived every morning to suck out the honey, as long as the cannas lasted.

We had a number of boating and swimming gymkhanas while in Imphal. Prizes were given for the boat races and the most ingenious means of crossing water obstacles with local produce. A lot of boats sank!

I can only remember one unfortunate incident taking place. At the end of a gymkhana we heard that a local man had been shot by one of our soldiers. The rifleman was arrested and the Manipuri rushed to hospital in Imphal with a bullet in his stomach. Later that evening the Brigadier ordered the I.O. and myself to go to the hospital and try to find out from the Manipuri what had taken place.

When we got there the operation had already started, however, we were told to enter the Operating Theatre and watch for a few minutes until the surgeon could talk to us. I knew the surgeon's father at Quetta. He told us that the man would be dead by 9.30 a.m. the next day. He died at 10.00 a.m. and we never had a chance to question him. The rifleman was tried for murder.

Chapter 17

Navvy

After a month in Battalion Camps, the Brigade went into Brigade Harbour with all its Units. Our Field Ambulance was commanded by the Doctor-Lieut-Colonel, I had last seen on a stretcher at the Armoured Brigade Dressing Station at Taukyn. We now had a full complement of men, Officers and equipment.

An area was selected at Mile 36 Imphal–Tiddim road. So far as we knew very few men had ever lived in this area, but it only took about ten minutes for the flies to find us; how did they know we were worth tormenting?

We had many schemes, including at least one set by Div. H.Q. in which 63 Bde. were the enemy.

Not far from our Harbour was a large lake called Loktak. As normal, the Staff Captain was asked to see if he could find two shot guns and some cartridges. He got them from an American Unit. The best was given to the Brigadier, while mine went to the Field Ambulance, where it was bound up with tape and shot, amongst other birds, the first goose.

After the Brigadier and I had spent a night in a Manipur house, done our own cooking and had a few duck to our guns, it was decided that Bde. H.Q. Troops should be given a chance to enjoy themselves. Every man was ordered to do his own cooking and to carry his correct weapons which included 2″ mortars. Boats would be hired and shooting would go on till breakfast. As far as I remember British Officers were spread amongst the flotilla. We sailed early in the morning and the first of a number of similar Sundays was founded.

Each man used his personal weapon to shoot at geese and duck. This lake was notorious for its wild fowl and for the fact that both eastern and western varieties of duck visited it.

We all got better at hitting our targets and I found that with a service rifle, with luck, one could bag a goose as soon as it rose off the water and showed a gap between itself and the lake. A lot of flukes happened but I never saw a mortar score a hit.

Three flukes took place on the same day. A member of my boat crew was one of the Brigade Clerks. Two geese flew over, quite high up. I said, 'Bet you cannot hit one of those!'

The Clerk took aim with his rifle, fired and a goose came down! The next two flukes were scored by me. After breakfast on the banks of a stream, a cormorant flew up-stream and my orderly said, 'Sahib, have a go with your revolver.' (Gurkhas eat cormorants.)

I did, and much to everyone's surprise I hit the bird.

Shortly after this episode the Brigadier said, 'See if you can hit one of those two pin-tail duck sitting on the water.' I borrowed my Orderly's rifle, then waded out to collect my duck, which had a deep groove on the top of his head and no other mark! The Brigadier said something which I cannot repeat and everyone laughed!

These weekend 'shoots' were much enjoyed and improved our home cooking. They were not without their repercussions. On one Sunday a convoy of M.T. were driving down the road to Imphal when they came under what they thought was enemy fire, which of course was our riccochets. They reported the incident on arrival at their base. Later that evening we were asked what we knew about this enemy penetration.

We replied that it must have been our Sunday shoot. No more was said, beyond 'keep clear of the road'.

During this period we started to have visits from a mobile cinema unit and also professional concert parties. Both were much appreciated and the live artists put up with a lot of very uncomfortable conditions, and the chance of infiltration by enemy patrols should they manage to avoid our position. I only heard one adverse comment about these parties and that was, 'Why do they think that we can only appreciate dirty jokes and double meanings?'

There were far too many of both of these forms of entertainment and we got very tired of it.

One day the Staff Captain and I.O. came to me and said, 'Do you realise that the Signals Officer is the only Englishman in Bde. H.Q.? It cannot be allowed to go on, he must become a Scot.'

I replied that I agreed with them and that I would take steps to ensure the

Signals Officer was elevated to higher things on St. Andrews Night, which was soon to take place. When the great night came George P. was brought to me, tried and found guilty of not being a Scot. His sentence was to be christened with Drambuie (which somehow we had) and to have a St. Andrews Cross scratched on his very bald head, then to be thrown through the Mess back window. The last act to ensure that George P. would enter the Mess a new man. Sentence was carried out amidst much laughter from us all, including George P., who was renamed MacPike of Torbung.

Torbung was a Kukie village not far from our harbour, who complained to their Political Agent that their economy was much at risk due to the amount of bamboo being cut down by our troops. The Brigadier sent our I.O. to visit the village Headman and to pay compensation. The reply he got was a very generous gesture of loyalty. The Headman and his Elders said that they were only too pleased to donate the bamboo as their contribution to the war effort.

By now we had our own 14th Army Newspaper and we sent the Torbung story to our newspaper, which the editor published.

On Christmas day 1942 we all enjoyed a cinema show, an extra tot of rum and Zu (rice beer or wine). At the end of the cinema show we returned to our Mess to enjoy our special Christmas ration of two hens. These hens were tied by their legs to a bush outside Sam's cookhouse. Sam, too, had made full use of the extra rum and was 'well away'. When the Brigadier saw our meal escape while being untied and run down the hill, chased by the other Mess staff, he went red in the face and told Sam what he thought of him. Sam became tearful and all he said was, 'Kiss me, Brigadier.'

What the Brigadier said I would not dare to record.

Dinner was not too late and the whole episode became a Brigade joke. We had various other parties such as Guy Fawkes night, when the men made images of the Jap Commander and let off thunder flashes and sticks of gelignite.

We had many visits from Senior Officers, including one from an Australian Brigadier who was serving under a great Australian General, who I knew in India and was known for his strong language.

During a talk our General said that our training was now quite different from anything we ever knew. In fact, he said it was no longer Training for War, but Training at War. We made as much use as we could of live ammunition, gelignite and thunder flashes. All conversations on the telephone were carried out by the use of what we called 'Baby Talk' and we always used code for important signals and any wireless used at night. We also learnt to make up booby traps and Molotov Cocktails, as well as bird traps and traps for enemy patrols which would give away their whereabouts in the jungle. The men soon learnt to take no notice of Jap Jitter Parties and never to open fire on anything but a major night attack. We learnt how to ambush and to kill silently. In fact, very soon we became a fighting force who treated the jungle as a friend. The only trouble was malaria; until some months later, when Mepacrin tablets appeared and all Officers and men were punished severely if they did not take their daily dose, the number of sick was too high. After the introduction of Mepacrin, cases of malaria in the Division dropped in a way which was very hard to believe, we all took on a yellow hue.

In the meantime, the road to Tiddim was slowly being made and it was decided that it must be pushed through by the monsoon.

5 R.G.R. were ordered to occupy Tiddim with a Rifle Company and a detachment of 3″ mortars.

A number of Commando Platoons from 70 Division joined the Tiddim Company and, aided by Chin Levies, raided into Burma. There were two tribes of Chins, the Haka Chins and the Falam Chins. One wore his hair in a bun on the top of his head, the other a bun at the back of his head.

The Chins were very useful as scouts and as a source of a number of ambushes on Jap linesmen and others. We had two characteristics which we had to learn. The first was that when they were issued with their first pair of Army boots they were unable to move!

The second was they worshipped their ancestors and at one side of an altar stood a pole from which were hung various animal skulls which in the after-life would be their slaves. A tiger skull was worth a lot. When the 5 R.G.R. Company first started their patrols, a rifleman who was leading an L.M.G. mule, tied the animal to one of these altars. The Chin villagers concerned said the mule must be killed as it now belonged to the ancestors. After a lot of arguing, and possibly some sort of compensation and threats, the matter was settled and we learnt not to do it again.

The Tiddim force was maintained on an 'all pack' basis and the work of the Mule Companies was most praiseworthy. Only mules could reach Tiddim at this stage. The road was far too steep for any vehicle and in places too narrow. There was also a fast and deep river to cross. The Manipur river required a good strong bridge. It was soon spanned by a Bailey Bridge as soon as the road could carry the bridging vehicles.

During February the Brigadier and I left for the Mile 109 area to select areas for Bde. H.Q. and the Brigade Units as orders had been received that all available troops would assist the Sappers in their task of road making.

We found some good areas and Bde. H.Q. was located on the banks of a bubbling hill stream which was dominated by a pink-blossomed tree and we named the spot 'Cherry Blossom Creek'. (It was probably an Almond tree.)

The road advanced daily and by the monsoon had reached a famous area which was called the 'Chocolate Staircase'. Unless one had seen this place after the first rains it would have been hard to realise what the mud was like. It moved in a steady thick mass down a very steep slope. It was impossible to believe that one day, in the not too distant future, our tanks would use the staircase.

Just after the conclusion of the Recce and allocation of areas to Units, I received orders to proceed on ten days' leave. Leave days or weeks counted from the time and date of crossing the river Bramahputra.

Units moved to their new locations in early March and operation Navvy got under way.

Joan had moved back to Ootacamund and was living in the hotel with our small son. So I made my way to Madras and then to Ootacamund for a very good leave, a lot of which was spent playing hockey with our energetic young child.

On the train back to Calcutta we were given baskets which contained a very reasonable dinner. The train was late and I, for one, very hungry so I said to the Indian Guard, 'Why are we so late?'

I was given the prompt reply, 'Sir, we are not late, we are twenty minutes overdue'!

I was met at Dimapur by a Brigade jeep and driver and returned to Mile 36 to find that the Brigadier had moved further up the Tiddim road to run a Weapon Training Camp. He left orders for me to join him the next day. However, I never got there as I was ordered to join the G.S.O.1 and to go to Shillong to start the Battalion Commanders and the Platoon Commanders School.

These two schools were under 4 Corps and my particular boss was the Senior Gunner Officer.

The Area Commander, Shillong gave me an area which was close to the Golf Course, on a well-wooded hill, with a splendid training area close at hand. The Senior School was about five miles from Shillong.

I got rooms in a Shillong hotel and prepared to move Joan from Ootacamund.

By now Operation Navvy was well under way and 17 Div. less 48 Bde. moved to Shillong for an operational 'let-up'. The let-up was a short one as 48 Bde. was in contact with the enemy at Tiddim and beyond Kennedy Peak and had just fought the battle of Basha Hill and one of the men of 5 R.G.R. won the Victoria Cross.

The Japs had learnt of Operation Navvy and found that he had a new road from Tiddim to Imphal and beyond.

We were all ordered back and I joined the 17 Div. Convoy and, after spending two nights en route, one of which was at 4 Corps H.Q. who were now located near Imphal Aerodrome. The Corps Commander was extremely kind and told his A.D.C. to ensure that I had a good packed ration for my onward journey.

I left early the next morning and decided to make the journey in one day, in the pelting rain as the monsoon had broken (May).

When we got to the Manipur river bridge, the Sapper Officer told me that it was up to me, but in his opinion the river, which was in full spate, would soon sweep away the Bailey bridge. I told the driver, who agreed, that we must risk it. This driver was a young Indian Mohammedan from the Div. M.T. Company, a splendid young man. I walked across ahead of my jeep which followed and we both got to the far side. So off we went up the hill to Tiddim in the rain and not having a clue where we were.

We got to Tiddim about 2.00 a.m. and found Bde. H.Q. where we both slept soundly.

The next morning I walked into the Brigadier's Basha and was greeted by 'WHA!' I somehow managed to keep the jeep driver?

I was soon in the general picture and the Brigade was ordered to plan a Brigade Attack supported by air cover against Basha Hill and Stockade 3.

By this stage the R.A.F. and Indian Airforce had been built into a very gallant, aggressive force, both fighter and supply. An area of Tiddim had been allocated for air drops and stores, etc., were being dropped to us in spite of the hazards of high mountains and very low clouds. One poor Tiddimite took a direct hit from an eighty-pound sack of flour and there was not much left of him.

One day during a talk to a Chin Patrol it was stated that a Jap head would be worth ten rupees — vast wealth to a Chin.

We had forgotten about the offer, when we heard that the Post Master of Tiddim had opened a C.O.D. parcel, addressed to the Commander of Tiddim, which was becoming a little smelly and no-one appeared to want the parcel. When the parcel was opened a Jap head rolled out, whereupon the Bengali Post Master fainted.

The Brigadier General staff of 4 Corps paid us a visit and told us that in the event of the Jap advancing in force and cutting the main road at the Beltang Lui area, we would have to cut across country and make for Aijal, which was about ten days' march across the grain of the country — a grand prospect!

The Brigade Attack was cancelled and I was ordered to return to Shillong as both schools were to be restarted.

17 Div. less 63 Bde. followed soon after and 63 Bde. took over Tiddim.

The Divisional Commander sanctioned wives to join their husbands provided they worked in our canteens, etc.

I was given an Army quarter near to the lines allocated to 48 Bde, who had been joined on a temporary basis by 1 Seaforth from 23 Div.

The Schools, were, I think a great success and we made full use of live ammunition and gelignite, etc., to toughen up newly arrived Officers and men who came from many formations other than 17 Div. I had a Platoon of 1 Seaforth and a Platoon of Gurkhas sent me as demonstration troops. Two incidents happened during the life of the School which are worth recording.

During a demonstration of what a battle field can look like, it was my intention that the students who felt sick should be sick there rather than in front of their men during the real thing. One of the spectators was an American General who turned to me at the end of the demonstration and said, 'Major, can I send some of my pansies on your course?' I told him that I should be delighted to see them.

Joan had decided to be one of my clerks in the School office as she could type. The other clerk was a delightful girl, daughter of the surgeon who had operated on my arm at Quetta and girlfriend of one of my Instructors. She was a member of the W.R.A.C.

The Senior School had a battery of 25 pdr. guns allocated for demonstrations and we a battery of 3.7 Hows Mountain guns. Both batteries had 'rogue' shells which screamed over their targets.

After one of the demonstrations described above, a 'rogue' shell burst well beyond its target. We did not worry about it as we thought that it was within the danger area. When I walked back to the School I was greeted by the Gurkha Sentry at the Quarter Guard with a handful of shrapnel and one or two expressions of a Gurkha nature! I went on to my office where the two ladies pointed to the roof which showed signs of shelling. Neither appeared to be in the least bit worried and burst into peals of laughter. Such were our womenfolk in wartime.

The two Schools closed down in October. I had some first-class young Officers sent to me as Instructors, who entered into the spirit of the School and of course all had battle experience. One of my Instructors I was to know as one of my Company Commanders some years after the war. Another was in a family firm of well-known publishers and another an international football player and a leader of a well-known dance band. All were grand men and I should like to have met them all again.

During our time in Shillong the Brigade lost the 4 G.R. whose place was taken by 9 Border. This meant a number of changes at Bde. H.Q. These new men had to be trained. The Brigade Commander published a training order part of which ordered that the Brigade, on one day per week (I think Tuesday), would 'turn night into day' and training, office work, etc., would be carried out at night and after a short break on Wednesday morning normal training would continue. This proved to be a most useful contribution to our retoughening and work as a Brigade.

We left Shillong, once again, on 7th December with the intention of carrying out some training in the area of Mile 54 road Imphal–Tiddim, but the enemy had other ideas so we moved direct to Tiddim.

The road had made great advances since the monsoon and was now fit for wheeled vehicles and supply by air had become a normal method of obtaining stores, mail, etc. We got to know the colours of parachutes used for numerous stores. I was the proud owner of a pair of red silk pants, made out of torn parachute used for dropping ammunition.

The road from Tiddim to Kennedy Peak was improved to a jeep road, then made fit for light trucks and eventually heavy vehicles and tanks. A wonderful piece of work by our Sappers and also the drivers, who at first had to drive with extreme care.

Soon the whole Division was concentrated at Tiddim. 63 Bde. were in the Kennedy Peak area and 48 Bde. at Tiddim. Enemy artillery and airforce became more active, but they did not cause much damage and never put the road out of action.

63 Bde were ordered to attack and retake Mile 52, Kennedy Peak — Fort White road, where the enemy had built a very strong (as we called it) bunker. We found later that this bunker had tunnels leading to it from well down the road to Fort White.

48 Bde. was ordered to thin out and be prepared to reinforce 63 Bde. if required. Bde. H.Q. moved to a bunker on Kennedy Peak from where we could see what was happening.

The 63 Bde. attack made little progress and the Battalion of 3 G.R., who tried so hard to oust the enemy from their bunker, started to take major casualties and their C.O. was killed. The attack was halted and 63 Bde. ordered to withdraw to Kennedy Peak.

The first tank had managed to reach Kennedy Peak and the next morning the young tank Commander was washing and found himself looking down on one of our aircraft. Such was the height of our battle position.

Our Gunners found that, because of our height above sea level and the mountain air, the range of a 25 pdr. gun was greatly increased. They were thus able to engage targets which should have been well out of range. This combined with our Gunners' accuracy and willingness to 'have a go' must have cost the enemy many casualties to personnel and transport.

63 Bde. was ordered back to Tiddim and 48 Bde. occupied the Dimlo–Kennedy Peak Area.

During the period that either 48 or 63 Brigade were in Tiddim, patrolling became a science and was very carefully planned and carried out. In fact, we became 'Masters of the Game'. Our Brigadier Commander was constantly considering patrol activity and insisted that long range patrols should live at Bde. H.Q. for at least four days before and after a patrol, where they would receive the best rations we could get, be carefully briefed or interrogated, learn to use a wireless set and a simple code. Their final briefing was given by the Brigade Commander or myself with the I.O. in attendance. 48 Bde. occupied a position with a steep slope down to a deep ravine. The Brigade Commander wished to know if it was possible for the enemy to climb the slope and attack our positions. He told me to take a Section of The Defence Platoon and find out.

I arranged to pass through the Baluch Bn. position at Mulben, and they kindly said that, before I left, they would patrol the area and tell me when this had been done. This they did.

All went well and, after a difficult scramble, we got to the top and reported the results to the Brigadier.

As a result of our patrol, every forward post or trench made a platform of bamboo, which overhung the slope. On this platform, large stones were placed, and the whole contraption was tied to stakes by string made of bamboo fibre. The string could be cut very easily by the use of a kukri, thus releasing the platform and its stones down the slope, and we hoped, on to the heads of any enemy who chose that route of attack.

We thus went back to ancient warfare, but one I should not like to face!

Air recce had reported a new enemy camp had appeared on the banks of the River Chindwin about thirty miles from Tiddim. We were ordered to find out what it was and the approximate strength of its occupants.

A patrol was sent off after a briefing by the Brigadier with the I.O. and myself in attendance. On the patrol's return I was told to interrogate the Commander.

The Naik in Command of the patrol started his story by saying, 'This is a strange war. The camp we watched was full of women.'

I asked him how he knew that the occupants were women and he replied that he didn't, until they marched down to the river and took off their clothes for a swim and wash. Later, during the advance back into Burma, our Intelligence confirmed that the camp belonged to a Japanese Comfort Battalion. Many of the girls said that they were given no option and had to enlist.

Other patrols did not produce such weird results, but everyone produced interesting and worthwhile results.

During the evening of 14th December, 1943, the Brigadier sent for me and said, 'Hand over to the I.O., pack your things and get back to Tiddim immediately and take over command of 1/3 G.R. in 63 Bde.'

I was thrilled at the thought of commanding a Battalion of Gurkhas, but felt very sad at leaving 48 Bde., where I had many friends and a Commander who I considered a superb leader in war. I next saw 48 Bde. when I was ordered to take over command for a vital battle as its Commander had gone into hospital. The Commander I knew had handed over and was on home leave prior to taking up an appointment in India, after having won three D.S.O.s for his very distinguished and gallant service.

My new Brigadier was a man of great ability but could not have been more different in either character or temperament to the one I had said goodbye to, after so many months.

Chapter 18

Tojo

Before continuing with future events, I feel that it is necessary to give some description of the country which was, in itself, a barrier to operations and a remarkable achievement by all soldiers who conquered it, especially the young British lads who had been brought up in towns.

Kennedy Peak is just under 2,000 feet in height and nights could be very cold. The Peak is part of the Letha range of mountains. Spurs of various lengths run up to the Letha and the 'grain' of the country runs north and south. Roads, at first, did not exist but, thanks to the work carried out by our Sappers and local Chins, a road was constructed from Manipur to Tiddim and to the top of Kennedy Peak. This road was capable of taking first jeeps, then light trucks and finally tanks and three-ton vehicles.

If a vehicle went off the road it could end up some 1,000 feet below, a very severe test for young drivers. Our patrols operated all over this country and down into Burma, in some cases a 'turn-in' of sixty miles.

My two Forward Companies on the Lophei Spur were 8,400 yards away as the 'crow flies', which was just in range of our 3.7 in Hows. The average time taken to reach Bn. H.Q. at Vangte by our forward troops, who were hill men, was seven and a half hours.

All ranks carried out their duties with full packs. In the monsoon the jungle was tropical and foul. Men were seldom, if ever, dry and the country was an ideal location for leeches which had many a meal off us.

Bad roads meant scanty rations. Local purchase did not exist and such items as eggs and bread were just a dream.

The supreme effort made by the Royal Air Force kept us fighting, but during the monsoon and other periods of low cloud, twelve days of air drops were good going.

We British were still getting soya link sausages, herring in tomato sauce and bully beef. Someone remarked that, just as he was going to sleep at night, a shoal of herrings swam passed his closed eyes, followed by skinless sausages which reminded him of naked babies.

There was no meat for Hindu troops as bully mutton or bully goat had, for some reason, not as yet been invented.

Morale remained very high and it would have been hard to have found a more cheerful spirit than that which was to be found in our Division, thanks to our General and his senior Commanders.

As I was driven down the road to Tiddim, I considered the situation with which I could be faced on arrival at Bn. H.Q. The Unit's Commanding Officer had broken down in health and his replacement had been killed at Mile 52. There was to be a new C.O. and Second-in-Command. Apart from all this, the Battalion had had a hard time during the monsoon first at Tiddim then at Fort White.

However, I need not have worried as I was immediately struck by the wonderful spirit and cheerfulness of all ranks. The new Second-in-Command came back from the Depot, I had been at school with him. Two experienced Company Commanders came back from leave and all other Officers and G.O.s had had a lot of battle experience and many of them I had known in Burma.

We soon got down to training and amenities for the men. The Subhedar Major was a great man and came from a sub-clan who were known for their amusing ways, but seldom if ever rose to Subhedar Major in peace time, due to the curious fact that they aged early in life.

However, the man who was my new S.M. proved to be young at heart and very sound in the advice he gave, as well as being extremely broad-minded over religious matters. Two other G.O.s were quite outstanding, brave and great leaders. The S.M. selected a Batman for me who had a nickname in the Battalion.

He was known as 'Dumba' after the fat-tailed sheep because of his broad backside. I had 'Dumba' for some weeks, but he was of the right quality to be promoted to N.C.O. status so he was replaced by another who was a Tamang, a 'clan' I did not know and did not enlist in Magar-Gurung Units.

He spoke a lot of strange words and, as I mentioned earlier, got a lot of fun teaching me to speak his dialect.

Div. H.Q. set a tactical exercise for us which we appeared to pass and we spent a lot of time concentrating on such things as moving silently in the jungle especially if big leaves were on the ground. These leaves, if trodden on, often broke with a loud bang which would give away the whereabouts of any patrol.

The lines were made as hygienic as possible and a tree rockery was built to which we transferred many specimens of beautiful orchids. A special prize was competed for by all Sections to persuade natural camouflage to grow on steel helmets. It did!

During this period many Staff and other Officers came to see us, including the Divisional Chaplain who I had met before as the Church of Scotland Minister of Simla. When I met him after the war it was in Lanark where he had a parish.

By January 1944 it became increasingly obvious that the enemy would have to make a move in some direction. The shelling from his long-range guns increased, especially at night, and he was establishing more large bunkers.

17 Div. ordered a really aggressive increase in our patrol activity. Mile 52 was now known as Mile 22 and it was raided several times. Medium guns were now supporting our two Brigades and a twenty-four-hour H.F. programme was carried out. By now the ammunition build-up was steadily increasing and we started to feel that we were no longer forgotten. Of course the Allies were correct to make the war in Europe the top priority, but it was bad for morale and difficult for our men to realise that their efforts would win or lose the war. A foolish bit of propaganda had been spread about, during a period when things looked very black, that we and our Allies had again landed in France. Whoever spread this rumour must have forgotten that reinforcements came to several British Units. They knew that such a rumour was impossible and said so, which made us very angry with those who had released the rumour.

We now knew that the enemy had prepared an underground fort on what was known as the Lophei Spur. We were ordered by 63 Bde. H.Q. to cooperate with a Frontier Force Regiment and to wire and booby trap the enemy into his own position, thus cutting him off from his supplies and water.

I had received orders that only two companies and some 3″ mortars were to be used, with two companies of F.F.R. Bn. H.Q. and two Rifle Companies, plus the remainder of our 3″ mortars with a battery of 3.7 Hows were to establish themselves at Vangte.

I detailed my Second-in-Command to the Lophei Spur Companies.

Vangte overlooked any advance by the enemy from the west. After a day or so a Baluch Battalion was ordered to establish itself on the right flank, which it did and carried out its task with distinction, winning a number of Decorations.

I had asked for leave to reinforce the Lophei Spur troops with another Rifle

Company but this request was refused. The enemy in their bunker got tired of being ambushed and, finding themselves running short of water and food and under constant bombardment by our 3.7 Hows, broke out on our right flank on the other Unit's front. It was this spot where the extra Company was to be placed and had been requested by my Second-in-Command.

One afternoon, about the 12th February, I was watching our Howitzer shells burst on the enemy bunker and reading messages from the Forward Companies, also Observation Posts, when I read a message from the Area Commander, Shillong, to tell me that our second son had been born on 10th February and that both my wife and son were well.

The Headman from the local village arrived one afternoon with his Field Security Officer and presented me with two chickens and said that he would like to come in and have a look round the Position. This man was suspected of cooperating with the Japs and I told him that no-one was allowed into our Position. I then thanked him for his present and wished him well. He went off to his village.

As soon as we knew the enemy had left his bunker I gave orders for the two forward Companies to explore the position and to destroy as much as they could and to booby trap any dug-outs they could not destroy. I learnt that one of the forward Company Commanders had been wounded by a booby trap and would have to be evacuated. Luckily his wounds were not too serious, but his evacuation would be felt as he was a first-class Regular Officer. All ranks knew and liked him.

When the examination of the Position at Lophei was completed the Second-in-Command reported that they had found a number of papers, ammunition, a dog and a skewbald pony. Included in the 'loot' was a letter addressed to the 'Commander of the Hill Fortress', an apt name as many of the chambers were twenty feet deep.

The Second-in-Command was ordered to return with the two Companies and arrived the next day.

We received orders that any men who were the recipients of decorations were to return to Tiddim to receive them from the Supreme Commander, Lord Louis Mountbatten. There was a full jeep load of men so I sent them off under command of the Second-in-Command as I could not leave Vangte.

When the men returned a day or so later I asked them what they thought of the Parade. Everyone had the same answer, 'We could not believe our ears when the King Emperor's relation spoke a few words and congratulated us in our own language.'

Stories such as this soon spread amongst the troops, British, Gurkha, Indian and African and we knew that we had a great leader.

Soon after this we were ordered back to Tiddim leaving the Baluch Battalion at Mualbem, where they repulsed several attacks.

Upon our arrival at Tiddim we were ordered to turn our 'lines' into a fortress which we started to do.

The pony captured at Lophei was given to me and carried my pack, amongst other things, during the withdrawal from Tiddim. The dog was adopted by the men and renamed Tojo. It went into many battles with the Leading Companies and would remain with them until the enemy medium machine guns opened up. Tojo then vanished, where to no-one ever found out, only to rejoin when the battle was over! Tojo had a special article published in S.E.A.C., written by a reporter, about his exploits.

The Manipur river flowed on to Burma away down the steep hill to the right flank of Tiddim. A good pack track was on the right bank of the Manipur and led to Mile 109, where we had established a supply base and hospital staffed by nurses. This track worried us but there were not enough troops to block the track and it had to be watched by patrols, until something had to be done to prevent enemy infiltration, which proved to be too late to stop a Japanese massacre of some of our base troops and also our nurses.

So far as I can now remember, it was during this stay in Tiddim that the Quartermaster reported that he had been issued with large tins of bully mutton. My Second-in-Command said that he had seen the tins but he would like me to inspect them and have a word with the Subhedar Major. I had a look at the tins, which were exactly the same as those used for bully beef, i.e. the type known as kerosene oil cans. I told the Subhedar Major I had been assured by higher authority that all tins marked as mutton were mutton and could be eaten by our men, but I added, 'Let's open one and see for ourselves what the contents look like.' He replied that he was quite satisfied by all that I had said and that he would tell me later what the men thought of it. The verdict was excellent and it made a very good curry. I had several meals from the men's cookhouse, enjoyed them all, and had no idea what the meat was, but knew it was not bully beef, which I had eaten so many times, cooked in every manner that the cook could think of!

The enemy continued the attacks on the Baluch Regiment in the Mualbem area but made no progress. A general enemy build-up was reported in the area Fort White–Mualbem. Artillery bombardment of Kennedy Peak increased and our positions came under fire from Jap 105mm guns which caused some damage on the first day but very few casualties.

Reports now started to come in of an enemy build-up to the west of the Manipur river and 3 G.R. were put at two hours' notice to move to the Tuibial Bridge, which spanned the river to the southwest of Tiddim, and we prepared to move. I put all my belongings in a small tin box, expecting to see them again on our return to Tiddim. We never came back, so once again I lost all my kit and such items as a spare watch. However, I did have all that I wanted, including a copy of A. A. Milne's poems I had borrowed from my son. The book called *Now We Are Six* contained a poem about the King of Peru which I read later on when reports were bad and I heard that the Battalion was either overrun or about to be. By the time I had read the poem I always heard that all was well! I also found that this poem helped me sleep at night. Why it did so I do not know, but it amused me and restored my temper to normal.

We were given orders to move on 11th March and to prevent any enemy infiltration across the bridge towards Tiddim. We moved after dark on the 11th and two Companies were sent over the bridge, while the Battalion less two Companies took up positions from which we could support the forward Companies by 3″ mortars and other weapons. On 12th March the Commando Platoon was ordered to pass through the forward Companies and occupy a position about ten miles away and watch the track and to engage the enemy if necessary. The Officer-in-Command of the Commando Platoon reported sick and was replaced by a very good Officer. I did not see the Platoon for a very long time, but they all returned having given very useful information and they also inflicted some casualties on the enemy.

On the 12th I watched an aerial battle between our Spitfires and enemy Zeros. These were the first Spitfires we had seen as they were new to the Burma Front. At first we could not make out who was who, but realised that the faster planes and those above the others were ours. The R.A.F. shot the Japs out of the sky and not many Japs lived to tell the story.

We were now getting reports that a large Column of enemy were moving along the Manipur river track heading for Mile 109.

63 Bde. were ordered with 10 G.R. to Tongzang followed by our B Company under command of our Second-in-Command acting as Company Commander, due to the absence of Company Commanders, one of whom was still being treated for his wounds received at Lophei, the other on leave. 3 G.R. less B Company were put under command of 48 Bde. and on the 13th March the evacuation of Tiddim started.

On 14th March 3 G.R. were ordered to withdraw at 1600 hours and report to 63 Bde. at Tongzang.

Just before we started our march the Commanding Officer of a British

Battalion asked us if he could march with us as he had orders to report to Div. H.Q. He told me that his Battalion had occupied our 'Lines' in Tiddim and were very struck by our hygiene and cleanliness, which was good to hear. To add to his surprise our Mess Cook produced an excellent meal when the Battalion rested for some food.

During the march to Tongzang we met our C.R.E. who told me that the enemy had established a road block at Tuitum which overlooked the bridge across the Manipur river.

On arrival at Tongzang at 1200 hours 15th March we found that Bde. H.Q. had moved to a hill which overlooked Tongzang and the Tuitum Ridge. This move which was unknown to me nearly cost the lives of two British Officers, my Head Clerk and the Battalion rum ration. One of the Officers was the Quarter-master. I had sent this mobile party on ahead to report to Bde. H.Q. and to find out where I was to go. They ran into the road block which they did not know existed. The driver of the jeep carrying the office and rum was killed.

I also found that B Company had been in action against an enemy position called Easy 14, had driven the enemy off the position and two of their men were awarded the M.M. apiece.

During the operation against Easy 14, B Company had killed a Japanese Officer and found in his haversack a document called 'Operation White Tiger', which proved to contain the outline plan for the main offensive on Dimapur and Imphal.

The Battalion had been located in the Tuitom area earlier on and knew the Headman called Paung Za Maung. The Second-in-Command knew this man well and knew that he was strongly suspect of cooperation with the Japanese. Paung Za Maung had a two-storied house with a remarkable lavatory with the seat located on the top floor and the pan at ground level. In the courtyard was a fish pond containing carp. A member of the Field Security lived with Paung Za Maung to keep an eye on him.

The Second-in-Command laid out our positions, locating Bn. H.Q. in Paung Za Maung's house.

Shortly after arriving at Tuitum village, I was ordered to report immediately to Bde. H.Q. where I learnt that a Battalion attack on the Tuitum Ridge, earlier in the day, had failed to take the position, largely due to an enemy medium machine gun located on a spur leading up to the ridge and artillery fire from the hills to the east. I was ordered to attack and clear the ridge the next day.

As I was returning to the Battalion, darkness fell and my Orderly and I had a difficult walk back down a goat track. When we were about half way down the track a fierce battle started on the road to Tiddim, about two miles from Tongzang, and we realised that Div. H.Q. was under attack, but we had no idea of the situation. The enemy got in but were driven off and all was well, we heard later.

I worked out a plan for our attack and ordered the Battalion to be on the move up the hill after the morning meal on the 16th and to get the maximum amount of sleep that night.

We had an excellent supper, which included some of Paung Za Maung's carp, and then we had a good night's rest.

Early the next morning firing broke out on C Company front. A Patrol from our British Battalion and a Jap Patrol met each other on the main road. C Company shot and killed a Japanese Officer who was also carrying important orders. Unfortunately the Japs killed two men of our British Patrol. The Japanese Officer killed by C Company proved to be an Intelligence Officer who carried several items of interest to our forces.

We moved up the hill and found ourselves on a flat piece of ground with an island of bunkers and stones in the middle. The M.M.G. spur led up to the ridge from the plateau. I gave out my outline plan, then allowed Company Commanders and G.O.s to have a good look at the ground and enemy position and ordered all concerned to be ready for 'Orders' at a certain time. All Senior G.O.s were ordered to attend 'Orders'.

Chapter 19

Back to Imphal

The attack started at 1200 hours after the air and artillery had pounded the enemy position. The enemy guns to the east were kept silent by counter-battery guns from our artillery.

During my orders I said, 'Remember the Sittang, it is up to us to pay back an old debt.'

I also ordered the Rifle Companies to attack in the Blitz formation which paid handsome dividends.

The leading Companies started off, led by Tojo. The medium machine gun soon opened up from its bunker on the slope. But it only fired a few rounds and wounded one man who died later in the day. From my command post on the stone island I was able to give the mortars their targets direct, one of which had been the enemy machine gun post. However, I could not see any men manning the gun.

We took the position and some prisoners, who were all ex-Indian Army men who had been taken elsewhere by the 'Nips' (Japs) and converted by them to fight against us and join Chandra Boze's Traitor Army.

These men were called J.I.F.s. Such Nips as survived our attack had beaten a hasty retreat.

One of my Gurkha Officers was telling me about the attack and a little later, when he said 'I looked into a bunker and saw two Jap men,' I said, 'Grand, we could do with a prisoner.' His answer was, 'What did you say about getting our own back and to remember the Sittang?'

I remembered. Whether he shot them or used his kukri I did not bother to ask, he had once again done a great job.

The machine gun was captured and on examination we found that one of our bullets had hit the gun and jammed the piston. We also found that it was fitted with a periscopic sight which appeared to be also telescopic and was of German manufacture.

When we had consolidated our position, I noticed movement on a hill across the main road. Bde. H.Q. were informed and told me that a Platoon from the 10 G.R. would shortly be sent me, come under command and would attack the hill.

Artillery were told to engage the Japs on the top of the hill, which they did with great accuracy. The Platoon took the position with ease. Unfortunately the Artillery were ordered to open fire again and wounded three of our men. I had quite a lot to say to the Brigade Major and told him in no uncertain terms to stop firing at our troops and only to order fire if demanded by me. The Platoon had done very well and had taken their objective in true Gurkha style and they had no further trouble during their occupation of the hill.

The Tuitum Ridge position yielded a number of weapons, ammunition, papers and our first Japanese Officer's sword.

We were also able to recover the body of the jeep driver, our office and practically 100 per cent of the rum ration. The jeep driver was buried near my new Bn. H.Q.

We remained on the Tuitum Ridge for two nights and Div. H.Q. moved to a temporary position between us and the river bridge, while 48 Bde. moved on towards Mile 109.

We handed over to 10 G.R. and gave them three anti-tank mines that we had been given.

We moved down the road, crossed the bridge and moved to the East, on the right bank of the Manipur river. We had just got to our new area when we were ordered to clear the enemy from what looked like a fort on top of a hill which overlooked the Brigade area. The enemy had established a strong point on top of a hill, known as Point 6247. It had been decided that the enemy should be ringed into his position and be starved out, by three companies, one of 3 G.R. and the others from two other Units. We were ordered to bombard the enemy position with mortar fire, which proved to be very accurate. During the bombardment one of our Royal Artillery Officers, who had been captured the day before, managed to escape and run down the hill to the path which led to it, just as our Company was moving into position. Seeing our men and thinking they were Japs, D.T. as he was nicknamed dived into a handy bush. One of our men saw him and shot him but luckily only wounded him. I went to see D.T. in the Field Ambulance to say that I was sorry for what had happened. I was told not to worry as he, D.T., was only too delighted to find he was alive, as he was certain that the Japs intended to kill him.

Meanwhile, the 10 G.R. were beating off all attacks made on them and 48 Bde. were heavily engaged at Mile 109 where the enemy had established themselves in strength after massacring all and everyone they could.

The 10 G.R. laid the three mines on the road to the bridge, just round a bend on the right of their position. Three enemy tanks came down the road and round the bend. The first blew itself up on the last mine, the second on the middle mine and the last on the first mine. Luck maybe, but that happens in war. Just after this event with the tanks, a large number of Jap Infantry were seen getting out of their lorries further up the road. Our Artillery opened fire and the first shells straddled the Japs and some lorries were set on fire.

One afternoon, the Subhedar Major appeared at my headquarters with two female goats which he had somehow acquired. The Gurkha does not like killing the female of the species unless he has to. I laughingly said to the S.M., 'Bad luck they are both females.' His reply was the equivalent of 'Says you!' So the G.O.s had one and the British Officers the other. No goat has ever tasted better.

The 10 G.R. were withdrew from Tuitum Ridge and the bridge was blown up. When the Ridge was clear of our men, the enemy moved up his artillery and we were shelled very hard over open sights, but with very little damage and very few casualties.

I think we remained on the river bank for about a week and I cannot remember what happened to the Japs on Pt.6247, but they did not leave their hill or cause us any more trouble.

We were ordered to withdraw from the river and acting under the Commander of the Baluch Battalion to act as rearguard. It was a tricky withdrawal as the Japs had the road under observation and well covered by artillery, especially a turn in the road called Windy Corner where, two days before, the C.O. of a Battalion had been killed by artillery fire. There was also a most irritating fighter aircraft who was determined to hit the O.C. Baluch and myself and we had to keep diving for cover.

Just beyond Windy Corner an ambulance was parked. I went to have a talk with the driver who proved to be an American. I asked him how he had managed to join one of our hospital units. He said that he had started off as a Conscientious Objector and found himself in an American Field Force Unit as a Medical Orderly, which was apparently normal procedure for people like him. He had managed to transfer to an Indian Field Ambulance. Now he said he would willingly join a Gurkha Unit and serve under British Officers. He then went to the back of his ambulance and pulled out three containers which were used for carrying 3″ mortar bombs.

Out of one he took some glasses, another a bottle of water and yet another a bottle of whisky having asked me what I would like to drink! He was a very tall man and just managed to fit in his ambulance where he spent the time reading comics.

I heard later that he had been awarded a decoration for carrying wounded off a hill and had applied for a Commission in a Gurkha Regiment. I saw quite a lot of 'Hank' as he was named, for a bit, but what happened to him I am afraid I do not know.

We got to Mile 109 after an eighteen-mile march and after a good night's rest were off again for Mile 105 to take over the position taken by 5 R.G.R. after a hard battle. Our Commando Platoon rejoined the Battalion at Mile 109 after many successful ambushes, as I have already recorded.

On the walk up to 5 R.G.R. we had to pass through the area where an Indian medium machine gun unit had been massacred by the enemy. Dead bodies were everywhere mixed up with abandoned machine guns. This area was on high ground and bordered the road to Imphal.

I sent out a Platoon Fighting Patrol under a G.O. who had been Jemedar Adjutant, an appointment I considered to consist of largely peace-time duties and the man concerned was far to good to waste. This Platoon did not get an opportunity to contact the enemy, but we were able to obtain some useful information.

The day after taking over Mile 105 the West Yorkshire Regiment was sent to me by M.T. I had been ordered to clear the enemy from the vicinity of the main road and the West Yorks to keep the road clear for the Divisional transport to withdraw.

I told my Adjutant to join me and we would see how a patrol of ours was getting on and if they had secured the start line for the West Yorks.

Our S.E.A.C. newspaper included a cartoon of a girl called Jane. This girl had managed to escape from some 'Baddies' and had to take refuge in a fountain, where she pretended to be a statue, which meant she had to remove her clothes. Poor Jane was stark naked and liable to be found by the 'Baddies' and there the cartoon ended for that day. Jane was a great favourite and none of us could bear the thought of anything evil happening to her. We had had our copies of S.E.A.C. and knew all was well with Jane.

As we were walking up the road, one of the W. Yorks' men said, 'Excuse me, Sir, do you know what has happened to Jane?' I answered, she was O.K. and at least a Company of Yorkshiremen said, 'Thank God, now we can attack in good heart.'

As we were getting near to where we hoped to find our patrol, firing broke out but soon ceased and there was no further trouble.

We were ordered to act as rearguard and to withdraw at 2300 hours after the Dumps, etc., at Mile 109 had been destroyed. The Company who had been employed keeping the Japs from bothering anyone else at Pt. 6247 rejoined us at Mile 105 and I recalled the Platoon which I had ordered to watch the west flank.

We withdrew on the third night after taking over the salubrious area of Mile 105 with orders to march to Mile 82 which was twenty-three miles of road which ran up and down hill. At Mile 100 we met our 3rd Bn. who had prepared breakfast for us all. They were part of 37 Bde. and had broken a Jap road block. I have forgotten which Division the 3rd Bn. belonged to. Our meeting and breakfast was a nice change, but of course we could not stay long. We reached Mile 82 and spent four nights there. We had been carrying our wounded and sick with us since leaving Tiddim, but now light aircraft were able to land and the casualties were evacuated. Mail was also flown up to us and a very black situation was avoided. I had left an order with a shop in Calcutta to send me two tins of tobacco a week. It had never failed until now and I found that I had only one pipe fill left. In the mail were two tins of tobacco. The Battalion issued a sigh of relief! We were attacked once without any damage and had to put up with a lot of shelling, but we suffered no casualties.

The air supply throughout our withdrawal had worked wonderfully well and we should have been in a poor way without it, especially at the bridge.

We were ordered to withdraw to Mile 41, a distance of forty-one miles. Apart from a long halt to cook a meal, we carried out the march with only the normal hourly halts and we were so fit that nobody was worried and, except for feeling tired, we thought that we could do a few miles more! Of Tojo there was no sign and I don't remember seeing him after Tuitum.

At Mile 41 we met a Bde. of another Division, spent one night and sent a Patrol out to a track crossing on our left flank, which I did not expect to be called upon to do, as the officers and men of my Battalion wanted a good night's rest. If I had expected this order I should have put the men of the patrol into our jeeps which were moving with us. I knew that my men would do the patrol well but I was fearful lest they were too tired to keep awake all night. In the event the patrol did their job and came in just after dawn.

We were told that we should be taken by M.T. to Mile 1 at Imphal where we should be re-equipped and receive some amenities. Our transport was assembled and then we heard that we were to form a defensive position at a place called Sengmai, north of Imphal on the road to Dimapur.

When we got to Sengmai we found a flat area with a curious isolated and well-wooded hill and the area nearest the enemy consisted of a semicircular ridge of hill connected by a steep ridge to the main hills.

The island was occupied by the remnants of an Indian Paratroop Regiment, about a Platoon of troops.

We were ordered to defend the right flank and took up our positions as ordered. The area had been occupied by some other formation and trenches, etc., had already been dug. Bde. H.Q. was located about the middle of the curved hill with slit trenches looking out towards the enemy. The rear was guarded by the Paratroops.

At about 2300 hours the enemy attacked my position but were driven off without much trouble and the rest of the night passed without incident.

The next day my two missing Company Commanders arrived back bearing with them a long tin bath. I was told how they had obtained it. I forget now how or where.

We were later ordered to change our position to the left flank to cover the ridge to the main hills. About half way along the ridge some formation had dug a Company position which was now unoccupied and a Company of ours soon were installed. I asked for as many anti-personnel mines as possible and these I received in time to lay them early the next day.

That night an enemy patrol attacked the machine gun post covering the ridge and were soon driven off. We had kept an M.M.G. from Mile 105, we should not have done so, but we did and never regretted our action.

Our Left Forward Company, commanded by the Officer who was wounded at Lophei, reported that the enemy had avoided the Company on the ridge and moved via the hillside, so we knew where to plant the mines.

The mines were planted in a large semicircle from the ridge downwards. That night the enemy made a stronger attack on our position, made no progress and tried again a little further down the hill and ran into the minefield, which he found difficult to avoid. The mines must have taken a toll of the enemy as there was quite a lot of shouting and they withdrew, never to attack us at Sengmai again. At daylight we found ample signs to know that the mines had done a good job. Exploded mines were replaced and the mine field extended and caught a small enemy patrol the next night.

The Company occupying the position on the ridge found that any attempt at movement on their part drew very heavy enemy fire from their position on the hill. I reported this to Bde. H.Q. which was being visited by the Carbineer Tank

Commander who came up to my H.Q. to have a look. He decided that if they made a real effort they could get two tanks up to my Company. The tanks, led by their C.O., made a monumental effort and by using 'block and tackle' got two tanks up the steep hill and the enemy withdrew before they were caught and made no attempt to attack us again.

The great battle for Kohima had started, in fact there was fierce fighting all the way from Sengmai to Kohima.

By now we had started to be issued with the American 'K' ration which at first we thought wonderful, but soon got fed up with the taste of spearmint, which seemed to penetrate through everything, including tins.

R.A.F. Transport Command continued to do a marvellous job and we were all old hands at air supply and soon got to know the capabilities of our fighter aircraft.

We had to put up with a lot of enemy shelling but suffered no casualties as we were, as a Brigade, tucked into the circular hills. We watched the shells burst on the flat area.

The long bath was located near Bn. H.Q. and was used a lot. It was rather fun to hear the shells whistling above our temporary bathhouse, which consisted of a ring of shrubs.

One very wet and blowy evening the Commander of A Company, the left Forward Company, phoned through to Bn. H.Q. and asked if he could have supper there. I said yes. I told him it would be from the men's cookhouse and would be curry and rice. He came down and dried off and then said he must get back to his Company — it was time to do so.

We never truly knew what happened, but came to the conclusion that it was something of this nature.

As this very fine Regular Officer neared his Company position on top of the hill, the Sentry challenged him and either the Company Commander did not hear the challenge or the Sentry did not hear the reply — we never knew.

The Sentry did the correct thing, he fired a shot in the direction of the noise he had heard and shot his Company Commander in the head. Sheer bad luck.

A second shot was heard and the young Sentry's body was found outside the barbed wire. He must have climbed over the wire and shot himself.

When I had heard of this tragedy I sent for the Subhedar Major, told him what had happened and told him to go up the hill and take command of A Company until further orders. I told the Senior G.O. of A Company what was happening and told him to meet the S.M. at his Company perimeter and said that I would see him the next day.

Robin, the Company Commander, was buried in the Military Cemetery at

Imphal. He had two brothers and a widowed mother in the U.K. Somehow the poor lady was told that her son had been shot for cowardice. How such a wicked story ever got out I cannot think. But I know that it did because one of the brothers, who was a Gunner, came to see me a few months later and asked me to tell him the true story; which I did and asked him to tell his mother, to whom I had written.

We were at Sengmai near Kanglatongbi from 2nd April to 5th May and made the place very secure.

Several plans were made and cancelled. One was to leave the 3 G.R., W. Yorks, the Para Platoon, some artillery and tanks at Sengmai while 63 Bde. less 3 G.R. moved to Bishenpur. The Sengmai force being under my command.

4 G.R. had left 17 Div. and were under orders of 32 Bde. They had carried out two very good attacks on enemy positions close to the Bishenpur–Silchar track. In the event a Brigade of 7 Div. took over Sengmai and I was ordered to report to 32 Bde. at Bishenpur.

I was given about a Platoon of 8 G.R. who had been in the area and allocated a sector outside Bishenpur overlooking the road Imphal–Tiddim. As the 8 G.R. men knew the area, I sent them out in a small patrol to search a wood with orders to come in at dawn, or before if the enemy were in strength. They came back at about midnight and reported a big enemy build-up in the wood towards the Loktak lake. I ordered the Bn. to stand-to and we waited for something to happen.

It never did. At dawn I sent out a 3 G.R. Patrol to search the wood, they reported 'All clear'.

Shortly after dawn one of our Artillery Spotter Aircraft flew up and the pilot decided to land in open ground near the wood. We did our best to signal to the pilot to get airborne again as there were possibly Japanese in the wood. He landed and then it dawned on him what our signals meant. He and his aircraft made a record take-off. These light aircraft, which were known to us as 'Cardboard Annies', did an excellent job not only for our Artillery but also as a means of obtaining information for us. The next night passed without incident.

At 1400 hours on 7th May our Brigade Commander arrived at Bishenpur and ordered 3 G.R. to occupy Potsangbam village just beyond Kwa-sipahi and the wood we had been watching. The operation was to be completed by nightfall. We started off at 1600 hours just as the light was failing using Kwa-sipahi and the wood to cover our advance, i.e. from the east. A Battalion of 32 Bde. had made two attacks on Potsangbam from the west and had failed each time.

Two Rifle Companies led our attack, B and D Coys. The rest of 3 G.R. were halted in Kwa-sipahi from where our 3″ mortars could support the two forward companies. I ordered O.C. B Coy. to take over command of the forward companies and coordinate any combined action and to keep me well informed of anything they decided to do, during the night. I also ordered three detachments of 3″ mortars to report to O.C. B Coy.

The two forward companies had advanced about 250 yards into Potsangbam when they contacted an enemy sniper screen and were halted until the enemy snipers had been dealt with. They then managed to advance a further 150 yards. I ordered the two forward companies to consolidate their position as it was by now pitch dark.

Patrols were sent out and reported a strong enemy bunker in front of D company on the extreme East flank and to the rear of Potsangbam.

When the attack started we were given the information that the enemy strength was only about one platoon plus. The W. Yorks made several valiant attempts to enter the position from the west, but had been beaten back with heavy casualties. I reported to Brigade and told them that the position was held by considerably more than a platoon plus, I also said that Kwa-sipahi must be held at all costs. I was ordered to hold on to what I had got and be prepared to attack the next day. Since our march from Tiddim we had had a Battery of 3″ mortars under Command and they greatly added to our fire power and became great friends, they were now ordered to join the W. Yorks.

Chapter 20

Bishenpur

The next day 10 G.R. took over Kwa-sipahi and we concentrated in Potsangbam.

We were given both tank and artillery support plus a call on air support.

The attack started with B Coy. right and D Coy. left. The advance went ahead until the leading Coys. reached a Nullah which ran through the village and proved to be a tank obstacle. The Nullah was bridged with a scissors bridge by our Sappers. B Coy. crossed the Nullah and reached its objective. But further movement towards the large enemy bunker, now known as S.E. Bastion, proved impossible. Two tanks were knocked out, one of which we were able to repair and D Coy. started to suffer heavy casualties. C Coy. moved up in support of D Coy. and we received orders to consolidate our position.

The scissors bridge was left in place and protected by B Coy. During the attack we had received very close support from the R.A.F. and the men were very impressed by their cooperation and help.

It was now decided that the Brigade should launch an attack on the next day with two Battalions, 3 G.R. right and 10 G.R. left both with artillery, tank and air support.

S.E. Bastion again proved to be a real problem and 10 G.R. were soon pinned down. Our A Coy. had moved to take over from D Coy. and started to take heavy casualties from S.E. Bastion and enemy 105 mm guns.

When we first entered Potsangbam, B Coy. were fired at by something very large in the way of a mortar bomb, which apart from a loud bang, caused no damage or casualties. It was never used again against us, but it was used against 48 Bde. as I will tell later.

I had a bad fright during one of the attacks! The pilot of one of our supporting aircraft signalled for us to show the position of Bn. H.Q., which we did. He then flew over again and threw out an empty beer bottle and we all thought that every 'Kelpie' in the world had descended on Potsangbam! The pilot then flew off with a wave of his hand — the young devil!

9 Border, two tanks and a mortar battery took over from W. Yorks. Our casualties were rising and by the end of the day our total had reached 150, including the G.O. who told me at Tuitum that he had carried out my orders and remembered the Sittang. I went up to see him on his stretcher and found that his wound would heal and I was more than pleased to hear this, as he was a most outstanding man.

A decision was made to leave S.E. Bastion, if possible, to starve and to occupy Potsangbam by night. 10 G.R. were detailed for the attack and 3 G.R. ordered to distract the enemy's attention away from the centre of the village and to give the impression that we were about to attack S.E. Bastion from the east and rear.

Our 'Dirty Tricks Department' had produced small fireworks which simulated a Battalion attack and the weapons which we would normally use. These fireworks were operated with time devices and so could be laid by a patrol some time before they were required.

We were sent a box of these tricks and told to place them to the east and rear of S.E. Bastion and to set them off to coincide with 10 G.R. advance.

Just as 10 G.R. were about to cross their start line we were attacked by a strong enemy patrol, but they were easily repulsed. But 10 G.R. wondered what on earth was going on as our 'Overs' were passing above their heads, but soon all was quiet again.

Then all hell broke out behind and to the east of S.E. Bastion and the fireworks started their 'Jitter Party'. 105 mm guns responded by firing a splendid and accurate D.F. programme. We had found that we were able to remove the bullet from captured enemy ammunition and these had been left at recent battle areas, minus explosive and with their bullets put back into the cartridge case. I hope that the Nips had many misfires!

10 G.R. got into the village and cleared another bunker called West Bastion. They handed over to the W. Yorks who boxed in and were rewarded at daylight by the sight of an enemy convoy of mules leave the hills to the West and head for Potsangbam with rations and ammunitions. They walked straight into the village and into the W. Yorks.

3 G.R. and 10 G.R. were ordered back to Kwa-sipahi to await orders. A most annoying Jap gun fired at any movement between Potsangbam and Kwa-

sipahi from somewhere in the hills, in the area of Kha Aimol which was separated from us by wet, open rice fields.

The monsoon had started, as this was now late May. We were not very far from Loktak lake and the water table was, therefore, close to ground level. Just about midnight I felt wet and found that I was afloat!

The lake rose and so did the water table. I was sleeping in a slit trench, but decided that I would rather face enemy shells than a midnight swim. I had to face neither alternative.

We had been ordered to advance to the hills via Kha Aimol village, which was to be occupied by 10 G.R. 3 G.R. were to lead the advance and establish a road block astride the enemy L. of C. on the top of the hills at Tokpa Khul.

We could not carry out a recce and no air photographs were available. The only two means possible were (a) to study the ground with field glasses and (b) to send out a recce patrol under the Bn. I.O. My I.O. in peace time was a Customs Officer at a distillery near my home. I threatened him with non-stop patrols unless he gave me a promise of duty-free whisky after the war!

The patrol had orders to move out on D night and stay on the ground until D + 2 night and to find out all they could about the enemy strength, location of their posts and the location of the gun which covered Kwa-siphapi and Pot-sangbam. This they did but were not able to pinpoint many posts, but there appeared to be several and a number of infantry guns plus the gun that bothered us.

The Brigade Commander had ordered us to cut a number of bamboo sticks which could be used to mark the road to Kha Aimol, using their white interior facing Kwa-sipahi. The attack was ordered to start at 1900 hours on a dry night at the end of May.

The I.O. and Intelligence Section led the Bn. and marked the route with the bamboo sticks.

All went well until we reached a Nullah at the foot of a steep rise. This Nullah was called the Charoikul Lok and, try as they might, the leading company which was A Coy. could not find the path leading up the hill to Kha Aimol. The whole area, in the dark, appeared to be covered with dense bamboo. To make matters worse we heard the alarm given in Kha Aimol. It was now about 0500 hours and would soon be daylight, so I decided to pull the Battalion out into the cover of another Nullah until I could see the ground and make a plan.

The 10 G.R. were just behind so I contacted their C.O. by wireless and we decided on the following plan.

10 G.R. would move on our left flank and attack Kha Aimol and 3 G.R. would find the track and take their objective on top of the hill.

As it became light the 'fun' began. The enemy had the Charoikul Lok well covered by L.M.G.s and the 75 mm gun. However, just before daylight we managed to find the entrance to the track which was a little downstream of the Lok and well hidden by bamboo, it also met the Lok at an angle.

Our plan was working and the 10 G.R. appeared to surprise the enemy and quickly captured the 75 mm gun. We found ourselves behind the L.M.G. posts and after a little firing by both sides, A Coy. pushed on and the enemy ran off into the jungle leaving their treasure chest.

A Coy. took the crest and two 3″ mortar detachments were put under their command. The position was wired and they also planted dozens of Punjis (sharpened bamboo spikes, heated in a fire). Every man and Officer carried a minimum of two dozen Punjis in their packs. These spikes were very sharp and would penetrate an Army boot. They varied in length and would give a nasty wound to a knee or shin.

The men soon dug their positions which were roofed with bamboo. I saw such a roof stop a 105 mm shell.

The enemy soon reacted to our presence and attacked us every night. One of their attacks was a very fierce one, but A Coy. held on and the attack was beaten off, after a small enemy infiltration outside the wire between A Coy. and the Company on its left.

The next day we collected eleven Officer's swords, many weapons and a large pair of scissors! We decided to give our R.A.F. friends some trophies.

The A Company Commander said that he would like a word with me about extra Platoons. I said that I would be up to see him as soon as I could.

Two or three days before this battle, I was sitting on the path to 3 G.R. position, from Kha Aimol, watching some reinforcements in order to welcome them to the Battalion, when an enemy 105 mm opened fire. As luck would have it, a shell hit a large tree on the edge of the path just as our men reached it. The shell exploded in the tree and took the stomach out of one of our men. I went down the hill and told the men to have a good look at their comrade and to both remember it and get their own back on the Japs in memory of their companion.

Just as I was about to start for A Coy. I heard a young Gurkha say he must see the Commanding Officer. He was jittering with rage and I have never seen a more angry man. I went out of my Command Post and asked the lad what the trouble was. His reply and subsequent present were not expected! He said, 'I was one of the reinforcements on the path when the shell hit the tree. You told us to get our own back. I was clearing the enemy who had got into part of the Company Position when I saw a Jap get behind a tree and threaten to throw two grenades. I then saw that they were not grenades but lumps of mud. I am not going to put up with such people as the Japs pulling my leg, so I drew my kukri and cut off his hands, which I have brought to you!'

We were a little worried about an elephant which was loose in the jungle between our position and the enemy. However, when the big attack started it moved off to a flank. We found later that it carried the large Jap mortar which we first met at Potsangbam and which fired some bombs at 48 Bde. I saw one of these bombs in the air and it looked like a tar barrel.

I went up to A Coy., saw the situation and called up a Platoon of another Company to report to O.C. A. Coy. We were not attacked again.

When we first came up the hill the plan was for 32 Bde. to advance and take over from us while we moved South and linked up with 48 Bde. This plan never happened, so we stayed where we were and 48 Bde. killed many Japs at their road blocks they were occupying at Moirang, Ningthoukong and Potsangbam.

32 Bde. were hard pressed at Bishenpur and elsewhere on the Silchar Track.

H.Q. 17 Div. was cut off by an enemy attack and road block at Oinam. There was in fact fierce fighting on all fronts. 2 Div. were advancing towards Imphal from Kohima. At this period Imphal was still cut off.

The road block at Oinam was broken by a Bn. of 1 G.R. under the command of an old Regimental friend, who was killed by a sniper. And supported by a Field Regt. R.A. commanded by a cousin of mine. I, of course, knew of both cases after Oinam was cleared and H.Q. 17 Div. were free to move.

We were ordered to withdraw from our position and take over the south front of Bishenpur, where the whole Bde. was ordered to take over from 32 Bde.

The night we withdrew was very wet and we waded through water on the track we had marked with bamboo sticks. 48 Bde. were engaged with the enemy on the main Imphal–Tiddim road. Their 'overs' were falling in the wet rice fields, but I do not remember anyone being injured by a stray bullet.

We took over our new area well after daylight when the Unit we were relieving moved up the Silchar track.

Both my I.O. and a young Lieutenant had originally come up from India and our Depot with a number of reinforcements. Both Officers asked to remain with the Bn. and I was given permission to keep them. Both proved their worth. The Subaltern knew about wine making and we soon had a 'distillery' working in our Mess. We found ginger growing in 'No Man's Land' and special ginger patrols were sent out. They also collected mango and other fruit. We found that a raisin helped fermentation and that we could not put a cork in a ginger wine bottle for forty-eight hours; if you did, it would explode. Our distillery soon became known in the Division and we were 'hard put' to meet our orders. Our General, especially, liked his ginger wine! I remember it was a powerful drink.

The R.A.F. Squadron which had given us such excellent support was located at a newly made airstrip towards Imphal. It was arranged that the Subhedar Major and I should leave Bishenpur one afternoon and present the Squadron with a few trophies, including an Officer's Sword. We paid them a quick visit, inspected some aircraft, had a drink and came back.

We had taken a lot of casualties and some destruction of equipment at our block on the hill and our strength was well down.

However, all was not 'gloom and doom' as a number of improvements had been introduced. Blood transfusions were very, very soon to be seen at Battalion level. Anti-malaria tablets had been issued and their swallowing by all ranks strictly enforced, with dramatic results. Vitamin tablets (C, I think) were also issued and all Officers below the rank of Full Colonel carried a rifle to make them less vulnerable to snipers. Bread had been issued and one day we were sitting down for some sort of lunch, when the Quartermaster arrived and said, 'There is fresh meat today.'

We thought that he had gone mad! He was correct. Our Senior Commanders had arranged for the Commonwealth of Australia to fly us direct so many days' meat and bread every week. What a change and how it cheered us all. The post was also working well, the real thing that worried people was the question often asked, 'If anything happens to me, will my family be O.K.?'

Chapter 21

Silchar Track

After a short rest at Bishenpur we were on the move again, this time up the track to Silchar. One morning I was talking to the Brigade Commander and O.C. 5 R.G.R. when we saw the enemy attack and overrun what was called Banana Ridge and Dog Piquet, a feature about three miles from Bishenpur. The enemy now commanded the Silchar Track and cut off 32 Bde.

We received orders to clear the enemy out of Banana Ridge and Dog. The approach to the enemy position was via a narrow 'neck' with steep Khud sides and it was not possible to employ more than a Platoon supported by mortars against the position. A 75 mm gun supported the enemy. We were quite high up and were able to locate the 75 mm. We had a troop of medium (5.5) guns at call, so we decided to direct them on to the enemy 75 mm. We ourselves (Bn. H.Q.) moved up to the track and our guns either mistook the ridge we were on as the one occupied by the 75 mm, or their shells had reached their ceiling. Whatever the cause the Adjutant, I.O. and I were blown off the track, but not one of us suffered any damage except surprise.

We moved forward to cover from where we could see the battle about to take place. We were leaning on a wall of stones when the 75 mm opened up. We got down but the I.O. was a little slow and pieces of the 75 mm shell went through the crown of his felt Gurkha hat, but he himself was untouched. His hat was the subject of much leg-pulling in the future as the I.O. refused to wear anything else, in the same way as I always wore the tin helmet which had been holed during the ambush on 6th March, 1942.

The Platoon attacking Dog Piquet was commanded by the Jemedar, who had been Jemedar Adjutant.

They opened the Silchar Track but failed to take Dog and suffered heavy casualties from grenades, mortars and enemy guns. The Platoon Commander tried several attacks until he himself was almost blown in two by an enemy mortar bomb.

Before this gallant man died he told his Runner to give me a message which I shall always remember. The message was, 'Tell the Colonel Sahib that we tried our best, but we could not move the enemy.' Thus died a gallant and faithful man and we all missed him.

We received orders not to attack Dog again, to leave it and keep the track free of enemy.

Now we experienced one of the medical wonders of the war. Close to my H.Q. I had my Regimental Aid Post tucked in under the hill. It was full of wounded and I learnt that most of them would receive a blood transfusion at the R.A.P.

Some of the men's wounds were very bad and I did not expect to see several of them again.

Thanks to the blood and the transfusion unit, which remained as part of all Bn. H.Q. for the future, most of the wounded were back ready to fight again in a remarkably short time.

We spent the night where we were until daylight when I knew that no enemy had infiltrated on to the track we held. Some men of 32 Bde. returned wounded, reported to me and I had a talk with some B.O.R.s who were very cheerful but worried by my orders not to let them any further forward till daylight. When I gave them a written message to their C.O. they appeared to be much happier.

We were ordered back to Bishenpur where we spent one night and then received orders to march up the hill and take over a position, in the clouds, from 4 G.R. The C.O. of 4 G.R., who I knew well, had recently been ambushed and killed by a Jap Patrol to the north of the Silchar Track, on the track to Khoirok. We took over from 4 G.R. who returned to Bishenpur area. We lived in the clouds with a battery of mountain guns and a battery of 3″ mortars. We spent the time sending out patrols and managed one very successful ambush.

We could hear sounds of battle on the Silchar Track, where the enemy was very active, also to the north of the track, facing the track and also in our direction. The enemy hung on to their positions in spite of repeated attacks by our forces. As far as we could estimate the enemy were in strength at about Mile 22 from Imphal.

We had realised three major changes in the enemy. One was, we could not get a prisoner as the Jap often carried a grenade strapped to his equipment and when wounded he would pull out the pin and blow himself up when approached. The second was, he would pretend to be dead and then shoot our man in the back. This trick infuriated the Gurkha and often meant a quick end to the Jap. The third and possibly the most important was the stripping of Jap dead of all their clothing and then leaving their dead on the battle field.

Up to now the Jap had taken every opportunity, for religious reasons, to remove his dead. Often after a battle the bodies were removed. We, of course, searched the Jap dead for documents, weapons, etc., and left the bodies where they had fallen and by daylight the next day they had gone. Now, as I have said, the naked bodies of Jap dead remained on the battle field.

We were ordered to carry out a 'sweep' and attack the enemy in the area of Mile 22 towards 5 R.G.R.

Our column consisted of ourselves, one Bty., 29 Indian Mountain Regiment (3.7 Hows) and 11th Mortar Bty (3″ mortars). We left Koirok under cover of thick cloud and must have loomed out of the mist and surprised the enemy, who were in very strong positions during the night. I could not see the enemy positions, but smelt them, so did everyone else. We had no battle as the enemy abandoned their defences and bolted down to the river which ran South of the Silchar Track. The area was covered with dense jungle, mostly bamboo, and it would have been difficult to deploy our mortars.

We soon discovered what we had smelt. The enemy had dug holes just large enough to take one man with little or no movement. These holes were in pairs and dug under the roots of clumps of bamboo and were nearly invisible. The Japs had been eating unripe corn and clearly had developed dysentery, but had orders not to leave their 'foxholes' for any purpose whatsoever.

We were glad to move on, past some Japanese dead, and make contact with a defended post manned by 5 R.G.R.

We arrived at Mile 22 with no casualties and came under command of 48 Bde., now commanded by an Officer who I knew well as commanding 5 R.G.R. and many years senior to me. My old Commander had been sent to India for a special appointment after some well-earned leave, a visit to various Training Schools in the U.K. and three D.S.O.s.

The new Commander of 48 Bde. and I got on very well together and understood each other. I gave him a full report of our 'sweep' and of the conditions we found. We both felt that things were not going very well with the Nips and thought that the Quartermaster side of their Invasion Force might be facing a breakdown and that they were short of basic rations and maybe ammunition.

After a couple of nights' rest we were, again, ordered to attack Dog and the end of Banana Ridge. During our first visit we had established a new strong point and called it Freddie Piquet.

We again took over Freddie and launched our attack. We soon started to suffer major casualties and I was ordered to call off any further attacks and withdrew to river Box, just outside Bishenpur, where the men could get a bath and wash their clothes. Freddie was handed over to a unit of 5 Div.

The Commander of 48 Bde. developed some illness, probably malaria, and had to go to hospital for a short period.

The men much enjoyed their time at river Box and had a well-earned rest.

I was now able to take in the overall situation and in general it was as follows, on our front.

The road Dimapur–Imphal was open as far as about two miles short of a village called Ningthoukhong Ka Kanou on the road to Tiddim and on the left flank to about Locheao on the road to the Kabaw Valley.

The Silchar Track, the road to Assam and thus to India, was still being attacked and was defended very stoutly by 32 Bde. and 5 Div.

It appeared, at one period, that the enemy were being reinforced along the hill track at Tokpa Khul.

A number of A.P. mines were laid at Topka Khul but the Nip found out that the village dogs were useful allies. The enemy rounded up as many dogs as they could and drove them ahead of their leading troops to set off the mines. We had spotted this trick when we were holding Tokpa Khul and could not think of any way which we could prevent it, except by getting our snipers to shoot any stray dogs.

There were indications that the enemy had been reinforced by a Korean Division. About a Platoon of these men, on our left flank, had risen from a ditch and surrendered to a Senior British Officer, who was on his way to watch an attack or some such thing. But there was plenty of 'fight' left in our enemy and their tails were only at half mast in limited areas.

We had been at river Box about two days when I received orders to report immediately to 17 Div. H.Q. north of Bishenpur. So I told the Second-in-Command to take over while I was away. When I got to 17 Div. H.Q. I was told that the General wished to see me. So I reported to him and was given the news about the new Brigade Commander of 48 Bde., which I have already recorded. The General told me to take over command of 48 Bde. immediately and be prepared to attack Ningthoukhong Ka Kanou in a few days' time, after I had formulated a plan. I should be given extra artillery and mortar support as well as air support for the attack. As soon as the first objective had been captured the Brigade was to clear the enemy from Thinunggei and possibly Moirang.

So back I went to 3 G.R. to brief my no. 2, collect my bedding and to set off for 48 Bde. H.Q. which was in a village on the road to Tiddim. There were two or three villages before Ningthoukhong occupied by 5 R.G.R., 7 G.R. and W. Yorks and one village unoccupied by anyone.

Bde. H.Q. was located in a well-made bunker, covered with a tarpaulin. Inside there were a number of half bamboo lengths making up a bamboo drain. Because of heavy shelling the tarpaulin had been punctured in several places and the pipe line saved the Brigadier and his staff from an involuntary shower.

During a quick look round, I spotted a stranger cooking our supper. I asked where Sam was and was told the very sad news that Sam was killed the day before by a shell. He was sitting on the wall of his cookhouse bunker, peeling potatoes, when a shell burst nearby and a splinter hit Sam in the head. I had known the faithful Sam for some time, he always had produced a meal whatever was happening and so often brought mugs of tea up to where the Brigadier and I were at the time, without worrying about enemy small arms fire, mortars or shells. His death was a sad loss to all who knew him.

I received information to tell me, that the Commander of the Supporting Artillery and Mortar would report the next morning when planning of the attack could start. I was told that I could have an extra Battalion if I wished. I decided to ask for 3 G.R. and ordered them to occupy the vacant village nearest to Ningthoukhong. The Battalion were due to have a number of strokes of luck and to enjoy themselves.

Two days before the attack was due to start, I ordered the W. Yorks to detail a strong fighting patrol to enter Ningthoukhong and harass the enemy. This patrol proved to be a most gallant operation, carried out with tenacity. The action of the W. Yorks pulled a number of enemy from their hill positions, destroyed an enemy tank and killed several enemy snipers. Unfortunately the patrol was cut off and their wireless batteries ran down. An air drop was carried out but a lot of stores drifted to the enemy. A Company of 7 G.R. attempted to relieve the patrol, their Company Commander was killed. The Patrol managed to get out of the village, but had lost sixteen men during their superb action. I had no hesitation in recommending two members of the patrol for decorations and was ordered to rewrite one citation for a V.C. Both men were awarded their original recommendations.

The 5 R.G.R. were selected for the attack and I requested that the O.C. 5 R.G.R. should be flown over the village and pick out likely trouble spots. This request was granted.

My Gunner Advisor suggested that we draw up a plan of Ningthoukhong, divide it up into areas, each area to be given a letter which could be used to obtain repeats of our artillery and mortar shelling. I decided to name the areas after my home town of Elgin. This left two areas without letters. However, you cannot 'stump' a good Gunner and I had a very good one helping me. He said we will call the areas T and RT, I asked why and he replied Tit and Right Tit and this is what they were called (see Map 4).

O.C. 5 R.G.R. carried out his air recce and reported the results to me and my Gunner. All plans were finished and the weight of shells and mortar bombs meant that saturation point would be reached in each area of Elgin, T and RT.

Battalion 3″ Mortars, less those of 5 R.G.R. and 3 G.R., were Brigaded under the Senior Mortar Officer and coordinated into the artillery plan. The R.A.F. were fully in the picture and given a plan of Elgin.

The Jap was expert in counter-attacking a position he had lost. These attacks came in at great speed.

This was allowed for in the artillery plan and an 'open barrage' laid on to be fired for half an hour quite automatically as soon as we had taken the village.

I was told to report, early in the afternoon, to a village on the main road, which was free from enemy shelling.

There, I met the Commander of 14th Army, Field Marshal Lord Sim. He had come up to wish me luck with our attack on the next day.

I very much appreciated the gesture and returned to my H.Q. with my morale very high.

Various people came to see me and talk over details for the next morning's battle.

The moon rose rather later that night and 3 G.R. reported some enemy tanks had moved up the road towards their position, but had now halted. A patrol of 3 G.R. confirmed that three enemy tanks had halted on the road, apparently waiting till the moon rose and they could see their targets. 3 G.R. had already taken ranges, of various objects, so the 3″ mortars already knew their ranges.

When the time came to 'open fire', one mortar bomb dropped into the open turret of a tank, and that was that! A second tank was put out of action by a patrol with an anti-tank weapon and grenades finished the crew of the third tank.

We had no further trouble that night from enemy tanks or attacks. 3 G.R. morale was very high.

The next day dawned without further rain and the programme got off to a good start. The road ditches were full of water, and after the barrage large ponds appeared and all retaining mud walls had disappeared, and no trees or houses were to be seen.

The Press were constantly asking to go forward, but I said no, until I knew that 5 R.G.R. had taken their objective, and that any possible counter attack had been repulsed.

When the Press were allowed forward, the photographer disappeared into the depths of a 'shell pond' with his camera and sank below thick muddy water and no film was saved.

The road ditch contained a number of bodies, all of which had beards. I presumed they were Koreans.

5 R.G.R. had two or three casualties, but dead enemy were everywhere. It was quite impossible for 5 R.G.R. to 'dig-in' so they waited for the anti-counter attack barrage to end, and then 'dug-in' on drier ground.

The next few days were spent patrolling and firing an harassing programme by our guns, on a co-ordinated programme with the patrols.

We actually got as far as Mulben, which, and its cross roads, had been bombarded by anti-aircraft guns, in a 'ground role'. Their targets were beyond the range of our guns.

We were ordered not to go further and to 'hand-over' to another Division and to withdraw to Imphal. The Commander of 48 Bde. returned and I was ordered to take over command of 63 Bde., whose Commander was evacuated to hospital.

Nothing happened in Imphal so I was told to go on leave and went to Shillong to join the family.

Chapter 22

Back to Peace Time — Almost

After a splendid leave in Shillong with my wife and two sons, the youngest of which was christened at the English Church, we all moved to Ranchi, where the Division concentrated. The hotel had been reserved for families, as wives were allowed to join their husbands provided they worked in the canteens.

I took over G.S.O.1 and the previous G.S.O.1, who was in an Indian Cavalry Regiment, took over command of 3 G.R. This move worried me as it was essential, in my opinion, that the C.O. of a Gurkha Battalion should be able to talk to the men in their language and not in Urdu. I know that other Indian Army Officers had been in command of Gurkha Battalions and had carried out their task in a very satisfactory manner. So I could only hope that this move, too, would be satisfactory.

My father-in-law had started his military career in the Border Regiment. The 9th Border's C.O. knew this and paid us the great honour of asking my wife to act as hostess at a drinks party given by the Regiment.

I found it very hard to settle into my new appointment and realised that three years of battle fighting and close contact with the enemy did not lend itself to a job which did not have direct contact with the troops. I am sure that it would not have taken long to settle, once one was dealing with soldiers at war. The General asked me one day if I was tired and I admitted that I was.

That Christmas we held a Divisional Headquarters drinks party. Many of the old faces had been replaced, many of the new faces had come from the Middle East and knew what battle was like, but they had still to learn what it was like to fight in a jungle and guns had to learn to avoid trees.

At the party were a number of Army Nurses and V.A.D.s. We were to get to know one of these girls very well, that is my wife and I, and I shall tell this story a little later on.

I soon heard that I had been posted as G.S.O.1 (Operations and Training) Headquarters Eastern Command, Tollygunge, Calcutta, India. I have reason to believe that I was asked for by my old Brigadier for another appointment connected with the training of snipers in the jungle. In fact I know I was. But the answer must have been, Not Available.

We left Ranchi on 31st December, 1944, for Calcutta. I took over my new job, quite expecting one day to return to 17 Div., as I understood that I was having what Lord Mountbatten termed an 'operational let-up' for those who had been forward for a long time.

We eventually were given a quarter at Tollygunge in the Indian Cinema Housing Area, which had been taken over by the Army, and very nice houses they were, quite up to the standard of film stars!

One of my tasks at Eastern Command was to allocate air passages to those who asked for them and to give each request a priority.

One day a V.A.D. asked to see me. She told me that she had met Joan and myself at the 17 Div. party. She also told me that she had just become engaged to a civil engineer in Calcutta, called John Perry. As a result she would probably be back late from leave. I was able to allocate an air passage for the next day with a reasonable priority.

A few weeks later the same girl came to see me and to ask me to give her away at her wedding to John Perry, who I did not then know. She said that I was one of the few people she knew in Calcutta. I said that I would and told Joan the story when I got back to my house.

The date, etc., was fixed and I turned up at the required time and place to collect the bride and Joan went direct to St. Peter's Church, Fort William, Calcutta. I had still not met John Perry. I spotted that the bride was very nervous, so poured out a strong brandy and soda and made her drink it.

When we were climbing the steps to the church door, Betty stumbled. I still say it was the brandy. Her story is that she had borrowed a petticoat, on finding out that her dress was transparent, and that when hitching up the dress to climb the steps she had forgotten about the extra garment. After the wedding service I went into the Vestry to sign the Register, after which I gave the bride a fatherly kiss, to be greeted by John Perry with the remark, 'Who the devil are you!' We then went to the Bengal Club for the reception.

In spite of John's remark we all became great friends and I had the pleasure of being John's guest at the Club and of meeting his Unit of the Auxiliary Force, all men who carried out their normal work and were on call in emergency. John was the Boss of Bomb Disposal and on call for any civil unrest.

The only form of operation I was involved in was planning for the Calcutta riots which we knew would take place, because none of the food was reaching those who needed it. The Buniahs were burying the rice, etc., to put up the price. As that part of Bengal is largely below sea level and the highest point is a mound of ten feet on the golf course, the buried food was soon going sour.

The Perry family and mine often saw each other and this continued long after the war and when we had settled in Scotland, when Betty and John came to stay with their daughter and son and Betty came up after John died.

Joan also died, so Betty and I decided on a sensible plan and married each other, thirty-eight years from our first meeting.

The only other outstanding event while in Calcutta was meeting our Malayan Prisoners of War, which included my own Battalion of 2nd Gurkhas. Their story was both touching and simple. Many men had undergone torture and never gave in to the enemy, including their Subhedar Major and the Acting Subhedar Major who took his place. Their loyalty and devotion to what was then the Raj was quite outstanding, like all our Regiments. I only hope the Gurkha gets his just reward.

I have already paid my gratitude to some of our nurses and I cannot end my war story without paying a humble tribute to the others.

My wife volunteered to join Lady Mountbatten's V.A.D.s for India after suffering, as thousands of others did, the bombing of London.

On the way to India her convoy was intercepted by German submarines and she had to experience the horror of seeing many Nursing Service friends sink below the waves. On arrival in India my wife was soon ordered to report to a hospital in the Chittagong area, together with other members of her batch. Illness prevented her going with the others, which meant that she remained alive. The Nips overran the Chittagong Hospital and murdered most of the staff regardless of sex.

I remained in Calcutta until the end of October 1945. The atom bombs had been dropped and the war was over. I just managed to see our daughter before leaving Calcutta.

I did not return to Burma, but instead joined my old Brigadier at the Small Arms School and a little later the New Infantry School.

I then came home on transfer to the British Service, thus severing the family connections with India which had been in existence since the days of John Company.

149

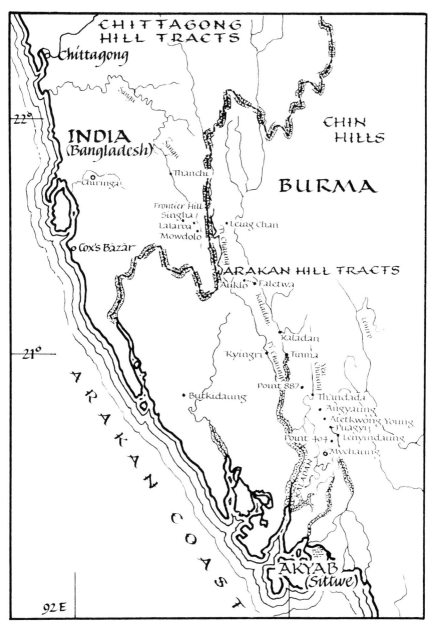

1. Burma, North of Rangoon

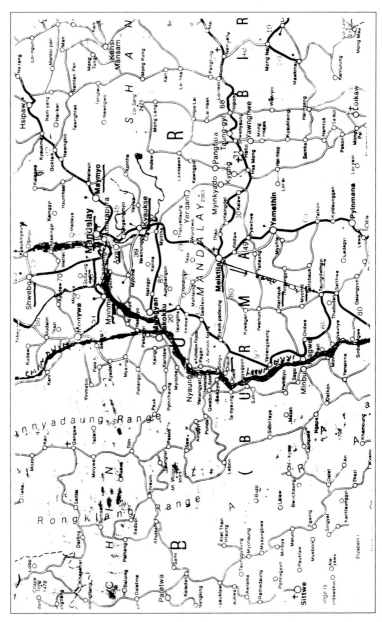

2. Mandalay, Maymo, Taungdwingyi

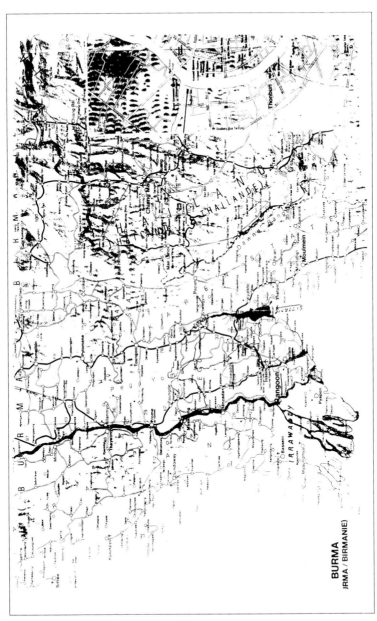

3. Burma and Thailand, showing the Sittang River.

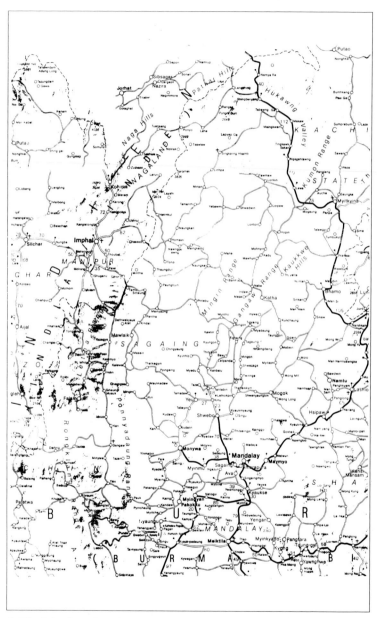

4. The Manipur Road and Imphal.